Testimonials

"Alex Lubarsky is a dedicated pioneer in the field of wellness, who is not afraid to speak his mind. When I picked this book up, I couldn't put it down. It's filled with simple, yet profound, strategies that can take both doctors and patients to a better place in life. I honestly believe that if the ideas in this courageous book are implemented, it can take our current healthcare system from up-side-down to right-side-up." - *Steve Rizzo, Author of Get Your SHIFT Together: How to Think, Laugh, and Enjoy Your Way to Success in Business and in Life.*

"In this groundbreaking new book, Alex Lubarsky shows how you can benefit while helping others achieve optimal health. A win-win for you and your clients! Can't recommend this one highly enough."-*JJ Virgin, CNS, Board Certified in Holistic Nutrition, Fitness Expert, Speaker, Media Personality and author of numerous bestselling books, including The Virgin Diet: Why Food Intolerance is the REAL Cause of Weight Gain.*

"It has been a privilege and honor to know and work with Alex Lubarsky for over 10 years. An innovator in the field of natural health and wellness, Alex's vision and creativity will influence the future of medicine and 'healing' for years to come. But *The art of SELLING the art of HEALING* goes beyond that: packed with savvy insights, funny anecdotes and moving recollections, Alex's book offers a blue-print of becoming a Man (with a capital 'M'), taking charge of his own life, and for the society he lives in. And this makes it a 'must read'. – *Sylvie Beljanski, President and CEO of Natural Source International, Ltd.*

"A first of its kind: a book written for the business of an emerging field of holistic, concierge & non-allopathic medicine with an autobiographical undertone. We get to take a look into what made the man behind the Health Media brand." - *Alex Shvartsman, DDS, ND, MAGD, IBDM, AIAOMT, author of Your Path to Healthier Dentistry: A Holistic Approach to Keeping Your Teeth for a Lifetime.*

"Alex has written a book that could be entitled *'How to Succeed in Establishing a Successful, Third-party Independent, Natural Medicine Practice.'* Many doctors are natural healers but never become successful, as they stay 'hidden' from the public. Successful marketing is not taught in medical school. Alex is not only an amazing medical marketing coach but the 'cheerleader and guide' in how to take action that we all need as well. This book leads us to that pathway to success, which I strongly recommend for all healers." – *Dr. Howard Robins is a world renowned expert in intravenous Ozone Therapy.*

"Alex is able to create a path for those he dedicates himself to that lays out a successful business in minimal time and money invested. Listening to his direction allowed me to go from zero to being known as the Expert in NYC in an amazingly short time. This book outlines the strategies and pitfalls which every Healing Practitioner must understand to succeed in today's marketplace. If your passion is to save lives and get your message out to as many as possible, find this book quickly and read it cover to cover."– *Louis Vastola, D.C.*

"The Art of Selling the Art of Healing is a 'sleeper'. I started to peruse the pages, but quickly got drawn into it cover to cover. A worthy read on all levels. Alex artfully blends a homespun true story of grit, determination and vision with life-enhancing wisdom and specific, easy-to-implement tips on how to support the health and sustainability of business. This organically allows practitioners to share information about natural therapies that increase the health of ourselves, our cells, our patients and our families!" - *Ellen Kamhi, PhD, RN, The Natural Nurse*® *author of numerous books, including Alternative Magazine's Definitive Guide to Weight Loss: 10 Healthy Ways to Permanently Shed Unwanted Pounds.*

"When I picked up the *Art of Selling the Art of Healing,* I was skeptical about it. What else am I going to learn from it? I thought that, after more than 30 years in medicine, I had a pretty good grasp on marketing my practice. But when I started reading, I realized that I was wrong. Alex Lubarsky's revelations about marketing not only gave me new ideas but also explained my mistakes. This is very important: to prevent mistakes in marketing. And there are plenty of them I made. But how to avoid them? Read this terrific book and find out." - *Sergey Kalitenko, MD, Anti-Aging and holistic medical doctor.*

"Through enlightening and entertaining anecdotes, Alex tells a great and poignant true story about health care in America from the unique outsider and insider's perspective. The relevance and plain insight from this master marketer will help every health care professional prosper from their core. In fact, everyone should read this book over dinner with their family!" - *Michael Berlin, D.C.*

"While in medical school and residency, we spend years learning how to save lives and heal our patients. Yet there are no classes on how to promote our skills and expertise. And so we, medical professionals, persevere on this path for many years giving our time and effort to grow as students of medicine. We practice with efficiency so we are able to heal as many patients as we can.

My desire to practice medicine and help people heal began in early childhood and has never wavered. Searching for the most authentic ways to heal has become my calling in life and I have dedicated myself to it.

I always assumed that being good at what one does will, undoubtedly, lead to a multitude of patients and I found this to be true. The rigorous training and focus that is required to become a physician does not leave much time for anything else, so not surprisingly, the business aspect of medicine had never crossed my mind. I was not prepared for the ever-changing healthcare landscape, the challenge of insurance reimbursement and the business end of healthcare. I found it necessary, in addition to practicing medicine, to reach out for resources to help me navigate this.

Alex is a savvy businessman who delivers a strongly-needed service. What he does sets a foundational precedent for the contemporary system of health care, a system in which various medical professionals become connected with the patients who are looking for more holistic healing.

We met years ago, while I was working at Dr. Linchitz' office. I immediately knew that his services would become invaluable to both medical professionals and patients.

The book you are about to read is the sum of Alex's many years of experience, in which he reflects on the successes and the challenges of my colleagues. It is both an informative and an inspirational read. As a result of reading it, both patients and medical professionals will benefit by understanding each other's side of a never-ending dialogue that is the process of healing." – **Natalie Cher, DO**

"*The Art of Selling the Art of Healing* gives you the insight on what it takes to make any business or situation successful. Great stories that share inspirational lessons with effective solutions. This book is a 'must' for any business owner or anyone looking to start a business." - ***Howard Hoffman*** *Founder of pHresh Products*

"Alex Lubarsky is a colorful character. He might be described as many things; part carnival barker, part impresario, part salesman . . . but, ultimately, I believe at heart Alex is a visionary. He has a clear and revolutionary vision of how to change healthcare in America from its current dysfunctional, non-patient driven, corporate reality to a system where patients can be responded to in a truly therapeutic manner and where doctors do not have to bypass a healing relationship with their patients in order to serve the dictates of insurance companies.

This book is essential for the consumer and the practitioner alike. It provides an invaluable roadmap through the often mad and disturbing world of healthcare. Read it. You're worth it!" - ***Dr. Garry D'Brant, DC, LCSW, DACBN, CTN, DIPl, AC***

The Art of Selling the Art of Healing

How the Rebels of Today Are Creating
the Health Care of Tomorrow; and
Why Your Life Depends on It

Alex Lubarsky

authorHOUSE®

AuthorHouse™
1663 Liberty Drive
Bloomington, IN 47403
www.authorhouse.com
Phone: 1 (800) 839-8640

Published by AuthorHouse 03/03/2015

ISBN: 978-1-4969-7070-1 (sc)
ISBN: 978-1-4969-7071-8 (hc)
ISBN: 978-1-4969-7069-5 (e)

Library of Congress Control Number: 2015903442

Table of Contents

To Rick.

Why This Book

Although for the last ten years my industry has been wellness, that is, marketing integrative doctors who focus on the underlying problem of a chronic condition and companies that produce health-supporting products and services, my experience in business (and marketing, in particular) has been fostered in a number of industries over some 30 years, primarily by starting numerous entrepreneurial endeavors from scratch, with no money, contacts or advantages of any kind.

After the 10th grade, my education has been mostly organic, without the miracle-grow effects of formal schooling. At the same time, my thirst for knowledge and my passion for life have lead me to reading over a thousand books and attending as many seminars and self-development courses. And although my spelling seriously depends on modern technology, my wild-crafted view of the world, business and marketing has permitted me to create something where there was nothing—to grow a garden, as it were, in the heart of a concrete jungle.

Other than a few months working as a stock boy for an Odd Lot store in Flushing, NY when I was 14, I have never held a job. I've never had a resume' or worked for a salary or received a paycheck. For better or worse, I have always been independent and have, over the decades, learned how to survive and even thrive in the middle of a vast, tumultuous ocean in a dingy of my own making.

It was about a dozen or so years ago when I accidently stumbled on to the wellness community, or as Paul Zane Pilzer, a renowned economist and author of *The Wellness Revolution* called it, the next trillion dollar industry. It was there that I met the most inspirational people in the world and watched as a few created very successful, multi-million dollar practices that did not rely on third-parties for payment and were strictly fee-for-service. And as they grew in stature and notoriety, I'd like to think that our efforts here at Health Media at least did not hinder their success and, perhaps, even helped propel it.

It was early in 2005 that we created our first public event now known as the *Nutrition, Aesthetics, Vitality, Efficacy, Life* (NAVEL) expo. It was relatively small, with four speakers, about six exhibit tables and some 30 people who attended on a Sunday afternoon that also happened to be the biggest snow storm of the year. Over the last decade, the event has grown to as many as 64 lectures, 80 exhibiting companies and thousands of people in attendance from around the world. We've hosted top keynote speakers like Suzanne Summers, Gary Null, Carol Alt and Dr. Mark Hyman to name a few, creating a platform from which to introduce our doctors to their best potential patient, and to build a channel of communication between the third-party independent healer, and the public that's looking for a more personal approach to care.

Doctors were always synonymous with entrepreneurship. Not so many years ago, most physicians were self-employed. It makes total sense. If you've invested so much time and money learning a skill, you want to enjoy the rewards that come along with it (not to mention be able to pay back the loans). It's not selfishness. It's not unkindness or callousness, and it does not make one egotistical. It's just human nature, and when harnessed, it has the ability to create the most good for the most people, including you.

Today, the average doctor is a slave to the masses—that great big blob of nebulous nothingness that demands she work on the collective farm and mostly donate her talents and hard-earned abilities for the greater good.

The reason for this book, then, is to share with the future generations of aspiring entrepreneurs and today's integrative wellness community, the iconoclastic idea that: *you don't have to be a slave to the system.* You have the power to create your own, and *now* is the best time to begin.

Marketing: Why None of It Works and How All of It Does

If you have been thinking about starting a business and you have no idea where to begin, or if you actually began to stretch your entrepreneurial muscles and find yourself in the middle of a desert; alone, scared, and under the heat of an unforgiving sun, I would like share with you some thoughts and hard-earned experience that was hot-poker-branded into my flesh and that may save you a lot of trouble, pain and unnecessary expense.

I began my marketing career on the streets of Ladispoli in beautiful Italy. I was 10 years old and, as a Russian immigrant on my way to

America, I sold all the knick-knacks that my family was able to pack in our suit cases; and that those lovely, eloquent and kind Italian people so generously bought.

Of course, I did not have much experience in sales, since in Russia commerce was illegal, and in Italy, I was just a kid. But I found myself to be naturally good at it. In fact, one of the things I was selling as I walked through the market past all of the traumatized immigrants of the former USSR (who were mostly professors, engineers, musicians and professionals of various kind) was a babushka head scarf that was very popular with the Russian women back home but, not surprisingly, a tougher sell in the fashion capital of the world.

At first I just stood near my parents who were manning a table in a row of a thousand other tables selling virtually the same things. It was a busy and loud market where, like a ballerina dancing with a bear, the harsh, clumsy vowels of "Da" and "Niet" of the seller tripped over the fragile and sexy "Si", "Benne" and "Gratzi" of their buyer. Mom wanted me close, afraid that if I wondered off I may be kidnapped by some well-dressed Italian, and since I was hoping I would be, I grabbed a stack of the head scarves and went out on my own.

It did not take long to figure out that even though I was selling the scarves at a slightly higher price, a price that I set myself, it was a much more effective way of connecting the product with the buyer and I sold out in a few hours. It wasn't just the scarf though; I came to understand later, it was me, with that scarf that got the attention of a prospective buyer. It was my proactive-ness, my willingness to step out of a comfort zone that I did not know I had, and take some risks that produced the above average results. I'd like to say that it was my fluid ability with the language, or my enchanting smile, but I did not speak Italian, nor did I smile. Because the only thing that resembled happy in the soviet block was a suspicious scowl, even when there was plenty of *vobla* and a fresh bottle of vodka to wash it down.

Stop Thief: Give Back My Doctor

The Health Care industry was stolen from the doctor, primarily because she was looking the other way when it happened. Sure she is busy, has lots of things to think about and there is a tremendous demand on her time. Doctors are also so medicine smart they get lost in the practicalities of business and, at times, life. Many will buy a large expensive home, but will never consider spending money on marketing their practice. They will lease a fancy car, but will try to build their business using word-of-mouth or social media exclusively. They sit night after night blogging, posting and uploading poorly produced home-made videos that do more harm than good. It is a top-heavy lifestyle and a neglected fuel supply that drives their business, i.e. marketing. That's what my friends in Texas call 'big hat, no cattle'. The Russians call it *pystoychainik*, or an empty tea pot, although I have no idea why.

More importantly, the reason I wrote this book is to make an effort to inspire the new generation of healers to take back the industry that they call home, and that is rightfully theirs, as well as the young entrepreneur to take action on her dreams even if she does not have the money, expertise or contacts to do it.

Imagine a time when the doctor, that remarkable human being who gave her entire life to learn how the body functions, what it needs to operate optimally and the mechanics of disease, is the one who has the final word on the system that maintains that engine of life, called "health"; when she calls the shots and makes the decisions that reflect on the health of the nation and the individual; when all third parties are set to the side and serve the doctors requests rather than the other way around.

If you ask why is our system of care so expensive, or why is our health as a nation so poor, or why do we wait to get sick before we think about being well. It is because third-party bureaucracies have pushed their way in between the patient and his doctor. In fact, they pushed passed sanity into zombie-like hypnosis. They have warped our system of care to be a profit center and not a healing center. They have stolen our system of *health* care and turned it into one of endless *disease* maintenance, because the doctor does not understand marketing and the practicalities of business.

In essence, doctors have been taught to fetch, and not hunt. They have turned the physician into a slave because he is afraid to stand up for himself and say "NO" to the self-serving insurance companies or the bloated and ever ravenous government agencies. He has given up all control, because he is unwilling to spend a portion of his income on reaching and educating the public on his philosophy about health. He has essentially given away his freedom because he does not understand how to turn on the engine that drives it.

In the next pages we'll discuss how to start that engine, put it in gear and gently press the accelerator, finding the perfect time when you can turn up the jam and put the pedal to the metal.

Something to think about: *The only limitations in this limitless universe are those that have been self-imposed on my mind.*

Chapter 1

Success in the Business of Wellness

"Completely accepting reality as it presents itself, is the essence of peace" – Richard Linchitz, MD

When I pulled up to the office, I already knew that this would be one of my bigger new clients.

I do marketing for a very small and very amazing group of people known as integrative doctors. They are physicians who were fed up working for relative minimum wage under the watchful eye of the Man, and decided go out on their own. That is a pretty bold move, primarily because you are not just opening a business like a pizza restaurant and going into competition with other pizza restaurants. You are going into competition with the United States Government, a large and ubiquitous bureaucracy that is hell-bent on getting involved in the health care business. Nay. It wants to be the health care business, itself.

It was a nice building in a prestigious part of town. They had an impressive looking website that I perused before making the trip. It had all the services that I had gotten very good at marketing over the last ten or so years. I was really just going in to finalize the deal based on the conversation we had on the phone and the assumptions I made in my mind.

As I walk into the office, I was greeted by a secretary who smiled and asked me to have a seat on one of ten expensive-looking chairs that fit the décor of this waiting room very nicely. I did. A few minutes later, the doctor came out to meet me. She had a lovely smile, a warm handshake and a pretty and kind face. We exchanged greetings, and I asked that she please show me around. It was a large space. Maybe twelve rooms, each dedicated to a particular function. There was a room for esthetics, one for the exam, chelation and intravenous vitamin drips, a room for supplements, and her office, where we finally ended the tour. There was lots of high-tech equipment and the space was tastefully decorated, exhuming an image of a successful doctor. It was perfect. For me.

As we sat down and began to chat, I asked her how she had gotten involved with integrative care and why would she leave the security of an insurance-based allopathic practice and start a fee-for-service concierge-type center. Unsurprisingly, it was a similar version of a story I hear repeatedly over the years; practicing as a standard medical doctor, operating in the standard system of third-party payments and disease management; all was well, except when she no longer was. And as this doctor began searching for answers to her own health problems, ones that her profession was not able to solve, she had to look into a place that perhaps she did not know existed, or did not trust, until then, that magical spot that contains all the wisdom of the world, her own sixth sense. She was about five minutes into her story when, all of a sudden, she stopped abruptly, broke eye contact, lowered hear head and began to cry. As the tears flowed, uncontrollably, down her cheeks, what started as a drizzle turned into a storm. And moments later, she was sobbing.

I just sat there waiting for her to regain composure, which did not take very long, just felt that way. She apologized. I waved it off. Concerned, I asked if she was ok. And here, through controlled tears and raw emotion, I heard the story that has changed my view of marketing, medicine and business forever.

The Horse Drawn Ferrari

During the oil boom, it was not uncommon for a farmer who was dirt-poor one day to become extremely wealthy the next. If one was lucky enough to have black gold discovered under his fields of corn, this fortuitous event would propel a backwards bumpkin into the ranks of the champagne-sipping, frock-wearing, mansion-dwelling elite, aka . . . the Beverly Hillbillies.

So it was an event of this kind that brought untold wealth to a farmer who took a small portion of his newfound cash to buy a brand new convertible Ferrari. As he was making his way through the main street of his little town on a busy Sunday afternoon, all eyes were on him. Not only because of the nice car he was in, but because there was no one behind the wheel as it slowly rolled down the street. He was sitting on the trunk, both feet resting on the tiny back seats, tugging on the reigns attached to the horse in front of the car, pulling it.

Most new business people make the same mistake. It is so common, and I've seen it so often, that I imagine this is the default way our mind works. I affectionately call it the *Flat Earth Fallacy*. It's how we see things . . . how we see the world. Only it's wrong. Dead wrong.

The engine under the sexy hood of that Ferrari is capable of generating 700X the power of that one horse. It could propel the driver down that road at a top speed of 370 mph, with the g-force so strong it would sink the back of his head into to the seat cushion, creating skin waves on his face. If only he knew how to start the engine, put it into gear, and step on the gas.

Most new business owners begin with this Ferrari Chariot version of their business. They spend all of their resources on infrastructure. They buy a nice office. (Because you can't have clients come to a dingy one.) They spend a fortune on building a website. (Because image is everything.) They hire staff, buy an impressive desk with a big, fancy, leather throne-like chair for the brains behind the enterprise, the best computers, and the very finest materials for the manufacture of their widgets.

Then for the next two years—or if the bank (or Dad) is willing to invest more money, maybe three— they sit there and wait for word-of-mouth to kick in, as they post more pictures of their six happy clients on Instagram and tweet this week's special to their 100 followers. Then finally, inevitably, they shut the lights, close the doors and forever give up on their dream of being an entrepreneur, as they slowly descend from the cloud of dreams into the dark, moldy and lugubrious dungeon of their former life.

And that is precisely what this doctor did. After receiving her training in Anti-Aging medicine from one of the largest and most reputable organizations in the country, this brilliant woman went out and bought the office space, hired staff, built a website and purchased the latest equipment and fine furniture. She invested everything she had and was able to borrow. And after two years of watching her financial reserves melt like an iceberg entering the Sahara, she finally gave up.

By the time I was sitting in that beautiful, expensive office listening to her painful story, there was nothing I could do. She was out of money, out of time and out of ideas. Worse of all, she was so depressed that even if she did have some of the former, there was no way she would be able to function effectively.

And that my friend is a big, tremendous, monumental loss. For her, for me, and for you.

The 30-year-old Flower Boy

When one of my relatives was 30, he resolved to open his own business. Most of his working life, prior to this moment, was spent as a car salesman. After going to a motivational seminar, where he was told that you will never get wealthy working for another man, he decided to strike out on his own. And on his way home, a couple of weeks later, he spotted the perfect opportunity. Across the street from a funeral parlor was a vacant store. This would make the perfect location for a flower shop considering that mourners paying final respects might want to buy flowers and wreaths for those they came to bid good bye.

So with all the enthusiasm of a kid who decided to run across a recently frozen pond, my relative mortgaged his house and did all the things you would expect an intelligent, new business owner to do. He took out a 5 year lease on the store, incorporated his business, got all the permits, insurance and licenses, built out the store with the latest refrigerated flower storage system and hired an experienced florist.

So far, so good?

This determined gentleman continued working his day job while running his business remotely, planning to leave once the business got going and he could make enough profit to replace the steady income his family has been counting on for the years prior.

It was a good, logical, well-thought-out plan. But it was wrong. Because after a year of coasting and passively waiting for enthusiastic customers to find him, he ran out of money, lost all of his investment, was forced to close the business, sell his house and move out of state to one where he could better afford his previous lifestyle with the added burden of a large debt.

So while you may never get wealthy working for another man, you will at least have a roof over your head and a shirt on your back. Just something to consider.

Thin Ice. Tread with Caution.

Starting a business is both an exciting and frightening proposition. It has all the attractiveness of adventure: driving your first car, seeking for hidden treasure or passionately kissing someone sexy for the first time.

The idea, for those who resonate with it, can generate all of the feelings and physical sensations of one of the most powerful motivational forces known to mankind, and one responsible for the procreation of the human race.

And if you actually succeed, then the promise of the good life—unlimited funds; time to do the things you've dreamed; the love, respect and admiration of your peers and of beautiful, well defined strangers—is almost impossible to resist.

But most people, who have never been in business and are bitten by the entrepreneurial tick, rush out and allow their senses to guide them through the rough seas; the hypnotic singing of the mythical sirens cause many a rookie sailor to shipwreck their vessel on the sharp rocks of inexperience.

Both the doctor and the florist in the above examples did everything seemingly r right. They did everything that I did the first time I embarked on this entrepreneurial journey and, maybe, what you would do as well. The only difference is that I started my first business before I had the responsibilities of supporting a family or paying a mortgage on a house that I could not afford; therefore, I had the luxury of time, as I flew headfirst into the walls within the endless roads of the success maze, learning by each painful mistake, navigating that extreme labyrinth bloodied, yet resolute, to find my cheese.

What Did You Say About My Mother?

My parents' main job was not making sure I became a wonderful and successful human being, just a live one. I am very grateful to both of them for the superhuman effort they made to give me a better life, one much better than the one they had at my age. Although both are remarkable, tough and loving parents who did the very best they could, circumstances made it difficult for them to do for their children everything they dreamed of doing when they were younger and starting a family.

As I share this part of my story, I'd like to preempt it with a short disclaimer: I love my parents and greatly appreciated everything they did (and tried to do) for me, their son. They had no choice in many aspects of their lives and tried to do the best they could with a deck devoid of any face cards.

My father's dad, my grandfather Leonid, was sent to a Russian *Gulag* for ten years. My father only got to see him when he was eleven and for a short time. Having contracted pneumonia in the brutal prisons of Stalin's USSR, and with little access to medical care, my dad grew up without a father.

My mom Adel (whose grandfather was a religious Jew with a religious wife, a long religious beard and 13 religious children—one of whom was my grandmother) also grew up just after WWII. Mom spent most of her childhood in a state-run boarding school, only seeing her family on special occasions. A smart, conscientious student, she did well in all her classes, including Atheism, where she had to prove why G-d did not exist. Her mom was a nurse and her dad was a partisan who fought behind enemy lines during that same war, with two bullet holes in his shoulder and lots of medals that I played with as a child.

My mom worked in a kindergarten and my dad as mostly a boxer, athlete and black-market entrepreneur. It was his five-year-old nephew (who was a child under my mother's care) that introduced them. Dad grew up on the harsh streets of post-war Soviet Russia. The youngest of four children, he was forced to dedicate his time to survival—for himself, his mom and his siblings. With food being the most important (and hard to come by) resource, the main focus of his effort was always to make sure we never went hungry.

The problem for my dad was that he was born an entrepreneur. It was in his blood and the way his mind worked. Sadly, he was living in a society that frowned on that kind of a free spirit. All of his activities, ones that would be handsomely rewarded in a country like the United States, carried strict fines and threat of prison when discovered. A derogatory label was even applied. Anyone who sold anything for more money than they bought it for was called a *spekylant; s*aid with a face of someone who just took a sniff of some spoiled milk.

Busy Bee and Don't Forget to Check the Oil

If I am ever in the area, I always pass by. On the corner of 7th Avenue South and Carmine Street in the West Village of Manhattan is where I cut my teeth on free enterprise. I was 19. Today there is a beautiful, relatively new building there; with modern condos, each selling for millions. In my time, a part of that lot of New York City real-estate was allocated to a tiny Texaco gas station. When I first saw it, it had been closed for over a year, mostly because the previous inhabitant fixed some cars, sold some gas, but made the real money by providing high-octane cocaine and sundries to the overstressed Wall Street gang a few blocks away.

I called it Busy Bee Auto Repair.

If you are going to start a business, it helps that you know a few things about it and you have some money to finance it in the high altitude, low oxygen beginning. Sadly I had neither. On top of that, I had no idea how to talk to people. Primarily because most of my teenage years prior, I spent kind of like Mowgly, that human boy who was left in the woods and reared by wolves; similarly, I was raised by taxi drivers, auto mechanics and the lovely, high-heeled "nurses" (as my father called them) who inhabited the streets of 47th Street and 11th Avenue in the 1980's.

They were all unique and beautiful people; some slightly bizarre, but most were good, hard-working, and hardly concerned about the niceties of language or rules. So when I spoke, I relied heavily on the "F" word with a peppering of UP, OFF and WHAT'TA, every so often, to break up the flow.

Certainly not groomed for customer service in dress or manner (nor was I certified by the Apex Automotive Repair and hardly knew the difference between a spark plug and a gas cap), there was no reason for me to think that I had a chance to do anything, but fail. Miserably.

It was just, I wasn't thinking that. I was bitten by the entrepreneurial tick and I saw nothing but Robin Leach and the wealthy lifestyles he portrayed so tantalizingly on one of my favorite television shows.

Don't Just Do It . . . Let Everyone Know You're Doing It.

Since I had zero money, I went to my new enterprise (a one bay shop with a tiny wedge-shaped office and a parking area for about five cars in the front) found a broom in the back and began to sweep. I cleaned it up and opened the gates, thus setting in motion the clock that would ring up $6500 dollars in rent, due the landlord at month's end.

That first week, I sold a few oil changes and a tune up, borrowing a mechanic from my father's shop to do the work. At the end of the week, I took the few hundred dollars that I made, went to the printer around the corner and ordered 10,000 flyers. As soon as I got them, (a day or two later) my girlfriend and I distributed them over a weekend and most evenings of the week that followed. A few months passed. I was able to hire a full time mechanic and buy a 10,000 piece circulation in a direct mail co-op, in addition to the flyers we distributed weekly. That was it. I had no personal overhead and really no expenses or responsibilities. I wore mostly t-shirts, jeans and sneakers. I didn't have a taste for gambling, clothing, travel or any of the finer things. So as my business continued to grow, I just plowed everything that came in back into marketing.

I tried every kind of marketing you can imagine: flyers, direct mail, custom- designed promotional pieces, calling on fleets, offering local garages and parking lots a finder's fee, promotions, discounts, newspaper ads, contests and publicity stunts. Once we offered to tow anyone home for free on New Year's night if they had a bit too much to drink, which got me in some newspapers and on *Good Morning America* and a bunch of radio stations. I bought large electric signs for the building that could be seen blocks away. I created incentivized referral programs for my happy clients, and I learned that the best marketing tactic of them all is to provide some added value that the customer isn't expecting so as to give my biggest fans a story they can share.

I arranged a deal with a local car wash and when a customer came in for an oil change, I would also have the car washed (at no additional charge and without saying anything about it). If there was a scratch and I could easily buff it out, I did that. If a bulb was out, I'd change it. Those kind of simple acts were no big deal for me, but it solved an annoying problem for the people who came to me and created the perfect environment for what was then known as *word-of-mouth marketing*; and today, it's *world*-of-mouth, as in the entire world, because social media permits a much larger reach than just those within earshot.

Once, a lovely young lady brought her car in for an oil change, and I noticed that in the dashboard of her car was a hole where the radio once was. Back then, it was not uncommon to have your car radio stolen. So I drove over to Canal Street to one of the many electronic stores there, bought an inexpensive radio and had my guys install it. She came back to pick up her car, paid for the oil change and began to drive off the lot, when she noticed the new radio neatly installed in her dash. She was literally stunned, and after expressing her gratitude, she became a one-woman marketing team who sent countless family members and friends to my shop. Turns out, she was a famous model and so were many of her friends. So, serving beautiful people kind of became my specialty. And all it cost me was $20 for a radio and a few minutes of a mechanic's time to install it.

Hey Buddy, What Do You Do?

It took me a few years of being in the auto repair business to realize that I was not in the business of fixing cars. I was in the business of marketing. It just so happened, at the time, it was marketing auto repair services. Most new entrepreneurs, who come into a creative project with an expiration date, may never learn this lesson. We'll just give it a year, they say. It breaks my heart to see a for rent sign on the dream of some brave soul who tried their hand at free enterprise but gave up a bit too soon. I did not have any of the necessary requirements on my entrepreneurial resume that would give me an edge against some of these really brilliant, highly-educated, well-spoken individuals who had their own cheerleading team behind them everywhere they went.

When I first opened that shop, I also had two partners who were older men and who, for many years, drove taxi cabs. They no longer wanted to sit behind the wheel twelve hours per day so they decided to get involved in a retail service business. At the time, I had just celebrated my 19th birthday, and both my new partners were ancient . . . in their late 30's, I imagine. They were married and had children, homes and overhead. When they stopped driving taxis, the income that they were making for the years prior stopped as well. So we were all in the same business but with drastically different motivations and realities.

As we all began to feel the pressures of the slow start of an underfunded enterprise, it did not take long for its two senior members to realize that it would not be something they were going to be able to sustain much longer, and without any idea of how long it would take this business to gain enough speed down the runway to provide the return they needed;

it was the uncertainty that deflated their spirits, and they both bowed out shortly thereafter.

Vision–Don't Leave Home Without It

The most important ingredient in the success of any enterprise (more than money, contacts or experience, expertise or luck even) is hope. Because as soon as we run out of hope, as soon as we cannot see or create in our mind a vision of the results we are thriving for, we become like the Norwegian rat that stops fighting for its life and drowns.

In an interesting (and somewhat cruel) experiment, scientists took a group of Norwegian field rats and placed them in a bucket to see how long they were able to tread water before drowning, and they discovered the one thing that made all the difference in the world . . . the difference between life and death, in fact. The first group of rats stayed afloat for about 20 minutes before drowning. In the second experiment, when the rat was exhausted and about to give up, the researcher would pull it out to safety and (after allowing it to rest) put it back in the same bucket. This time, thinking that the rescue is imminent, the rat would tread water for some 36 hours. Big difference, and an important lesson for would-be entrepreneurs. With hope, you have everything; without it, you drown.

Fear Is the Real "F" Word

It gets even tougher when you go into business with the burden of an expensive lifestyle you've build over the last 10 or so years. It can be like swimming across the Hudson as you make a stroke with one hand and hold up your trunks with the other. A house with a big mortgage, children in private school, a homemaker who prefers leisure, a couple of leased BMW's, two vacations per year and all of the charities, birthdays and holiday obligations . . . you have a lot to lose if this endeavor goes south. And try to tell your spouse that you're going to risk this burdensome fairy tale lifestyle to pursue the passions of your heart. Tell them that you need to temporarily downsize, so you have the resources and time to build something that reflects the deep, raging undercurrent of your vision, your passion and, ultimately, a real world expression of your true self.

So I meet professional people all the time who are expressing their entrepreneurial endeavors more like a hobby; one that they think about in between their full time job, family obligations and televised sports. It's the businessman's version of a tethered hot air balloon ride. You get in the basket, go up the few feet that the rope attached to the spike in the ground below permits, and come back down. It's pretty safe and very boring. It has an element of fun but not nearly that of actually untying the rope and flying towards the sky.

Richard Branson, one of this century's most celebrated facilitators of numerous global enterprises, describes his hot air balloon ride around the world in his inspiring book *Like a Virgin: Secrets They Won't Teach You in Business School*. It was marked with danger, life and death decisions, and an environment that tapped his deepest motivation, creativity and quick thinking. It also speaks to the reason for his remarkable achievements in so many disparate and unrelated endeavors. He is willing to untie his proverbial balloon and then push it to the limit of possibility. In the end, discovering just how far it can go because he took it to places where it would go no more.

There Is No "Plan B"

Standing on a two-inch thick wire, between the two towers of a ten-story hotel in San Juan, Puerto Rico, a 73-year-old Karl Wallenda ended his spectacular five-decade, high wire career with a five second fall to the ground below. Prior to that tragic event, his name was synonymous with a world-renowned troupe, known for their heart-pounding aerial feats and the fact that they did not use a net in any of their acts. On the one hand, it was the reason for Karl's deadly accident, and that of a number of his family members over the last 200 years of walking the wire. On the other, it is the element of death that makes the pursuit of adventure so exciting, both for the performer and spectator.

In his book, *Life on The Wire: A Story of Faith, Family and Life on the Line,* Karl's grandson Nick Wallenda, explained why his family members did not use a safety net, not even during practice. Some years ago, a member of their troop fell off the wire on to the net below, bounced off and fell to the ground breaking his neck. Certainly a safety net can save your life, but it can also create a false sense of security, permitting you to let down your guard, become lax and lose that edge. So instead of a net, the great Wallenda's utilize the greatest of all safety tools: intense and fanatical preparation. Knowing that there is no net paradoxically creates one.

Although very different than walking a wire, when I did my radio show, I much preferred to do it live. Certainly having an editor on my side going over a pre-recorded show, removing anything that would make me look less than polished only seemed to produce more things that needed editing. When the show was live, however, there was an energy flowing through my whole being, electrifying my mind and creating a sharpness that was simply not available in the safe, pre-recorded option.

My Problem Is Your Marketing Opportunity

Recently, I spent four glorious days in Isla Verde, San Juan. I stayed at the magnificent Water Beach Club; one of the most relaxing boutique hotels, on one of the most tranquil paradise islands that is still the United States. I was there to meet with the hotel management to discuss marketing, so I went alone.

After spending about two hours under the tropical sun, slow-roasting my bone marrow and making some organic vitamin D, I went upstairs to my room for a shower and a nap. (Very important at my age, I'm told.) I woke up, picked up the novel that I was reading, and immersed myself in the story as the stress of the last ten years of relentlessly building an enterprise began evaporating off my soul. I was deep into the story of the spy thriller when I heard a faint knock on the door. I got up, tightened the belt on my thick, white, WBC monogrammed robe, and walked over to see who was there.

I was expecting no one, so my New York alarm bells began to ring. If ever so slightly. When I opened the door, there was a very attractive young lady standing in front of me. She had a trim-fitting black dress, outlining a lovely figure. Her lips were a shade of red that was pronounced but not overbearing. She had straight black hair lightly gelled and combed back, and an olive complexion that was not uncommon on this tropical paradise. I did not say anything. Neither did she. She just looked straight in my eyes with something of a confident mischief. Finally, as her lips began to form a smile, revealing her pearly white and very straight teeth, she said, in a form of a question: "chocolate!"

"I'm sorry, what?" I asked.

"Would you like some chocolate?" She answered as she extended her arm with two mini chocolate bars perfectly displayed on the palm her delicate hand.

"That is exactly what I was hoping you'd say," I replied with a smile as I collected my gifts, reluctantly closed the door, and went back to reading my novel, with the residual taste of dark chocolate lingering on my taste buds, and a lovely memory forever etched, on my mind.

Carmen, as her name tag explained, worked for the hotel. Her job was to make those who stayed there feel welcome and special. With that simple and personal gesture she was able to add a neon sign to all the other wonderful, but expected things set to background. Modern room, beautiful view of the endless, turquoise ocean, clean, high thread-count sheets, nice bathroom, good food at the hotel restaurants, and easy registration and check out service. We've come to expect good service in a good hotel, but add a personal touch, like a couple of unexpected chocolates and you have all the makings for a winning marketing program poised to generate some world-of-mouth.

This is remarkable because it's unusual. It's inexpensive, but the value, in this world of social media, can hardly be measured, where anyone in the world can hear and share your story. This story. And, this is what I call *World-of-Mouth* marketing.

Guess Who. No, Really. Guess.

Walking the historic streets of Old San Juan, I passed a store selling brand name clothing. I won't mention the brand, but you can guess if you like. As I walked in, I was greeted by the usual young fashionista who offered to help me. I declined because I knew exactly what I wanted. Two pairs of jeans, 31 waist by 30 length, straight cut and as simple as possible. It took me all of three minutes to find them; another couple to try them on and, in short order, I had my money out ready to pay for the purchase. Simple. Fun. Done.

It was about a month later, back in New York that I noticed the fancy button on the front of the jeans, which I really liked and fitted me well, was coming loose. Being someone who never takes things back or calls to complain, I was ready to add these really cool jeans to the donation bag. Then I decided to do something that was totally out of character for me. I called the company. I called during the business hours the recording that asked me to leave a message outlined. Later in the day, I got a call back. I answered the phone, and the person on the other end began explaining that if the purchase was not made in one of their brand stores, there was nothing she was able to do.

Now, really flexing my dissatisfied customer muscles, I asked for the manager. It was after about eight minutes of listening to some hip music/brand self-promotion, that the manager finally said, "Hello. May I help you?" "Yes, please," I replied and began to (once again) reiterate my story. "Ok," said the manager, "Why don't you take a picture of the button so I can see what happened, and email it to me with your proof of purchase." I did. A few days later, I received an enthusiastic email reply: "Yes, we see the damage, and it is very unusual so we are happy to send you a replacement button, and we will also be willing to pay for the repair. Just send us the invoice."

Here is how the rest of the conversation went in a form of an email:

Dear Kelly, thank you so much for your offer to help.

First, it's the material that is ripped, and the new button would have to be moved over to one side, or higher or lower, with a gaping hole in a somewhat prominent spot.

Second, quite honestly, I am not enthused to take the time to go and drop these jeans off to be mended and then go back and pick them up. Usually I would have already put them into the Salvation Army bag, and that, would be that. I am however very interested in the story. Soooo . . . !

Having already made two calls, and stayed on the phone for 10 minutes, 8 of them waiting on hold, I've probably invested more than the average person is willing, just to rectify a simple and sundry issue.

So, here is the story again, and in more detail.

I have owned a pair of jeans ever since my family came to the United States in 1979. At first it was hand-me-downs, then mostly a no-name brand, then Levis and the like, now I can permit myself the luxury of a more expensive option. And over the years I have either worn-out, ripped or ruined many a pair. This is however, the first time that a button has torn through the jean itself.

So, if sending a new button is the best you can do for a first time customer of your brand, then this completes my inquiry, and I greatly appreciate your time.

I would have you keep in mind that in today's market place, simply having a big budget to reach the masses and ignoring the needs of existing clients, is a about as good a strategy as polishing the brass on the bow of your lovely boat, when the hull is rotting and taking on water.

To your great success! – alex

Well, you get the picture. Now, what would happen, if when I called, someone actually answered the phone? And when I explained the situation, they would similarly request a photo of the damage, and once they saw that their brand was compromised, immediately offered to send me a replacement pair with a coupon for 50% off a future purchase. The answer is fairly simple. They would have had a customer for life, and one who would have shared this shockingly awesome story of service at every opportunity. But it was not to be, and I will never purchase this brand again, and instead share this un-inspiring story to serve as a warning for all of us who aspire to thrive in our chosen endeavors.

Having unlimited resources for marketing was always the way large corporations shaped opinion and created belief systems that would ultimately become the impetus for the kind of actions that would best serve its goals. So, if you have indigestion, how do you spell relief? If you are like most TV-watching American masses older than a two cell zygote, then it's R-O-L-A-I-D-S. And that's how it's done. If you can consistently place your message on the only three TV stations, or a handful of radio stations, or the only newspaper in town, then it's a fairly simple model. First, make a product, then sell the product, after that take the profits and market the product. As you sell more, you market more. That's all. Easy, peasy. And then it's gravy.

Today, it's very different. We have television, yes. But there are a thousand channels. We have radio stations, but we also have Pandora, and iTunes, and podcasts, and newspapers and YouTube and Google, and blogs, and a billion websites. The world of reaching the consumer has changed virtually overnight and the process is growing exponentially. Is it that difficult to imagine 10,000 TV channels in the near future? Or a million?

The point is that the power of marketing has shifted from mega-corporations to the consumer and the creative entrepreneur who serves them. When a company spends billions on advertising a slogan, but gives someone a run-around for a $50 purchase, they are creating the perfect environment for a city-size sinkhole just below their fancy office building.

An Entrepreneur's Most Valuable Tool

If a train leaves from Moscow at 7 am traveling a distance of 400 km, what time will it arrive at St. Petersburg at the speed of 40 km per hour? As a kid I loved these kinds of math problems. When I found them, I would spend hours trying to solve them just for fun. But for an entrepreneur, there is a better riddle, one that I just have to invite you to ponder. How much money will you make next year, if you are deathly ill the next? It's a bit more difficult than my train problem but much more important to consider.

For the last 15 years, I had the distinct honor of working with wellness-oriented physicians and the many authors who discuss healthy living protocols. And although this book is focused on marketing, I would like to take just a few sentences to discuss how important your optimal health is in your overall success and how much you can affect its consistent presence over the duration of your career and life span.

So many people who start a business leave their wellbeing for something they will worry about once they achieve whatever it is they are after; so they eat poorly, they don't exercise and expose themselves to chronic, health-destroying stress, without taking the time to decompress every so often. That is just so wrong. You are nothing more than a combination of a few trillion cells—brain cells, muscle cells, nerve cells, and ultimately how well those cells function (and whether they have the quality materials necessary to create the next generation of cells) will play a big part in how well you think, the quality of the decisions you make and the energy you bring to your endeavors. In the most practical sense, you need your health to succeed in business and in life, but you will also need it later, once you create whatever it is you are building and want to enjoy some of the fruits of your labor.

A terrific book by Pat Williams—*How to Be Like Walt: Capturing the Disney Magic Every Day of Your Life*—shares the story of Walt Disney at 62 saying that he will accomplish in the next 20 years more than he has done up until that point. In fact, the original idea for Disney World in Florida was to be the city of the future where people used the very latest technology and lived in a laboratory of sorts for the cutting edge of every industry. Sadly, Walt passed away a few years later from lung cancer resulting from a three-pack-a-day smoking habit of the unfiltered

Lucky Strikes, his favorite cigarettes. And we, as a society, will never know just how much we lost because of it.

The road to success is usually longer and more difficult than you think or plan for when you begin. So it's very good advice to make provisions to last through some of the inevitable long stretches of famine and cold winters. Take walks, drink the best quality water you can find, see a wellness doctors, and get a stand-up desk so you don't sit yourself into a heart attack. Breathe deeply, know your vitamin D levels, work out with weights, get massages, eat your veggies, take your vitamins, and get a whole house water filter. Also "do a little dance, make a little love, [and] get down tonight."

You will succeed. It's inevitable, if only you play with that kind of attitude as a given. And don't burn yourself out and destroy the most important engine that drives your entire dream.

So the answer to the above riddle is, five pm, and it is 'health' that is the most important tool of the entrepreneur. And that, is all I have to say about that.

Social Media Is a Fad

If you and I wanted to get to a hockey game in Manhattan from Suffolk County say, we can hitch-hike and get there for free, or we can pay the three shackles and take the train. Either way we will most likely get to see the Rangers lose. Certainly there are no guarantees with either choice. We can be kidnapped by some loon who picks up strangers, or we can be shot by one on public transportation. But, if we were to make a calculated risk, then I think paying the few bucks for a train ticket will in all probability get us there on time and with much less trouble.

Most rookie business people, however, will do anything possible to try and thumb their way to success. Anything that is free they will spend countless hours doing, but when it comes to actually paying for marketing, it's like trying to convince a philanthropic debutant to mud-wrestle for charity. She really wants to do it, but something is holding her back.

I really can't relate.

Marketing, advertising and publicity allowed me to build each of the many businesses I started. It is imperative to spend a portion of your original start-up resources to breaking the inertia and creating some crucial momentum as you pull the throttle to full speed and give it everything you got to assure liftoff.

Once you have built a platform of recognition, all of a sudden opportunities begin to find you. It is an interesting paradox; when you need it most, no one wants to give you the time of day. But as soon as you are busy and in high demand, all of a sudden everyone wants to talk to you.

During a recent lunch with a concierge doctor, as we were getting to know each other, he confided in me about the affluent lifestyle he established and was trying to maintain even though the original source of income dried up some time ago. Now, having gone into his own fee-for-service practice, he was using networking and social media to get his practice off the ground while pulling that heavy sled of static overhead. And at the same time trying to outrun the very likely risk of the last grain of sand falling through the hour glass and the game ending as his finite resources run dry. Well, if we think about this tactic in mathematical terms, then the numbers add up, but only when we're celebrating our 200th birthday. This way of developing your business takes forever and its practicality and cautiousness are fraught with danger of failure by risk aversion.

Let's say you networked with 100 people. How many of them actually know what you do? How many like and trust you enough to try your services? How many believe in your philosophy and will be satisfied even if they do come to see you? If you are an integrative, concierge doctor—one who charges cash for services—I would guess, maybe, you'll get one out of that 100. And they come to you as if they are doing you a big favor. You are on the defensive, afraid to say the wrong thing to upset them so, walking on eggshells, you try extra hard to make sure they are happy with you. But if you are in high demand and a client is about to stick a hairpin into a wall socket, you're not afraid to slap some sense into them.

If, however, through marketing you reached out to 10,000 people and the same ration applied, then you have 100 or so potential patients who have to accept your terms. You are free to be yourself; your word carries more authority so people are more apt to follow through on your suggestions, producing better outcomes. And the fact that you are busy, creates the perception that you are successful, and don't need any one individual patient. So demand grows and they start saying my doctor is so good I can't even get in to see her.

Now the momentum picks up steam and your core group of satisfied clients refers to you the same high quality clients. This is the Tornado Effect that will take you to Oz. That place of mystery, abundance, fun, happiness and satisfaction, known as success.

When You Don't Need Marketing You Need it Most

One of my very close friends is a brilliant entrepreneur who, over the last twenty years, established retail stores in virtually every mall throughout the tri-state area. For many years, his business did well. Yet anytime the topic of marketing came up in our conversations he always said that he does not believe in it and has never done it, although his business has always thrived. And it's true; there are certain instances where marketing is really not necessary. Yet those are probably also the situations where it is needed most. The thing my friend failed to understand is that, although he did not need marketing (or believed in it) the malls that drove the traffic to his stores spent a fortune trying to reach and motivate people to spend their weekend shopping there. How? Through word-of-mouth? No. By doing consistent marketing through every imaginable media channel. So as time passed, the malls continued to raise his rents, cutting further into his profit margins. Eventually, they we're able to choose more profitable options of name-brand stores and made it more difficult for him to function, leaving him completely at the mercy of a merciless bureaucratic blob.

Similarly, for many years, doctors felt that they do not need marketing, primarily because the insurance companies would drive more patients to their office than they knew what to do with. And in the beginning, doctors were reimbursed well and all was good with the world. Today, that same mindset is causing lots of pain for the health care industry.

Doctors who grew up in this model just don't understand that the insurance companies spent a large portion of their resources on marketing and selling people to join their network and pay a monthly premium. And since they controlled the flow of patients they also controlled the market place. Over the years, insurance companies precipitously cut reimbursement and made the physician jump through the fire hoops of death just to get paid for services rendered. And still, most doctors will try to function in that antiquated system and refuse to even look out of the box, let alone think out of one.

And don't get me started about the Indian-giving government health-insurance programs, structured as generational Ponzi schemes that come back and demand that you return years-worth of payments they made to you because you did not dot the "T" or cross your "eyes" as they so clearly explained in their 100,000 page manual beset with contradictions, dead ends and stupid mind-numbing bureaucracy.

Turning the Page

If you got this far, I imagine that at least you see that something is definitely wrong with the fundamental system of health care, even though everyone is telling you that if you would just work harder, then eventually, *Arbeit Macht Frei* or "Work Shall Set Your Free." So let's take a look a multi-faceted marketing program that will help tip the seesaw away from the self-serving bureaucrat to the healer and, ultimately, the patient.

Something to think about: *If the customer is always right; you don't have enough customers.*

Chapter 2

The Greatest Salesman I Know Is My Doctor

"I am here for a purpose and that purpose is to grow into a mountain, not to shrink to a grain of sand. Henceforth will I apply ALL my efforts to become the highest mountain of all and I will strain my potential until it cries for mercy." — Og Mandino, The Greatest Salesman in the World

The sun was directly above the freshly dug grave surrounded by the family and friends of a remarkable man for whom this would be the final resting place. It was near a large imposing tree standing guard and, perhaps, sharing the many stories of lives lived. If you listened close in the somber silence of the moment, you could hear the soft wind blowing through its leaves, whispering something that we could not understand, even if we tried.

It was a loss felt by everyone there. And it was difficult to find a bright spot in this tragedy, to find a semblance of fairness or to explain why. This was a painful and deflating experience for me and the hundred or so ashen faces in proximity.

Sitting in the office of his oncologist 14 years prior, he finally received the long-awaited diagnosis after months of unexplainable symptoms that were making life miserable.

Broncho-alveolar carcinoma.

An aggressive form of lung cancer that required surgery to remove an egg-shaped tumor from the lower right lung followed by all the standard treatment protocols of chemotherapy, immune-suppressing drugs and radiation. "Three to five years, 50% survival rate," was what his doctor said before callously leaving the room and closing the door behind him.

It was a bleak moment in a flurry of bleak moments in recent past.

If we rewind just a little bit, however, Dr. Richard Linchitz (or Rick, as he preferred to be called) was a successful medical doctor, board certified in pain management, neurology and psychiatry, who for many years ran a thriving pain management practice with some 40 employees. He was a tri-athlete who could have moonlighted as a fitness model, and (if that's not enough) he was brilliant. Graduating Cornell Medical College in the Alpha Omega Alpha Medical Society and married for over 30 years, Rick was the very proud father of three children and (more recently) two beautiful grandchildren who were the joy of his life, permeating every aspect of it.

Sitting there in the office of that oncologist, Rick became angry and resolute at the same time. He decided that he would not allow someone else to dictate the terms of his life and searched the world for the answer to his precarious situation. This would be the fight of his life and he was going to take it on as he did any formidable challenge that he's ever encountered—head on and with all he had. After the surgery, Rick decided to forgo the other standard treatment options suggested, primarily because his own research showed that it did little to affect his particular type of cancer, while substantially reducing quality of life.

When I first met Rick, he was just celebrating his 55th birthday . . . and the third disheartening post diagnosis anniversary. Doggedly refusing to satisfy his doctor's prognosis, he looked and felt exceptionally well. His search for answers brought him to become certified in medical acupuncture, Anti-Aging medicine and Insulin Potentiation Therapy (IPT—an innovative cancer treatment used successfully for over 30 years by Dr. Donato Perez Garcia, a third generation physician, currently practicing at the Medical Consultation Tower in Hospital Angeles de Tijuana).

Dr. Garcia's grandfather (also a medical doctor) realized that cancer cells thrived on sugar and would open their many receptors when they sensed that it was ingested into the system. Using this as the basis for his protocol, he would inject insulin into the patient followed by a glucose solution and, at the right time (when the cancer cell is most vulnerable) deliver a tiny dose of chemotherapy, filling the damaged cell with up to a 1000 times the dose of the drug, completely destroying the mutant cells without damaging any of the healthy ones. At the same time, he would use immune boosters and detoxification so as to strengthen the immune system and remove all interference, creating the perfect environment for the body to heal.

I was invited to meet with Dr. Linchitz at the office he recently opened to treat other cancer patients, mostly friends of friends, who heard of his unlikely recovery and asked for his help. It was a tiny, one-room space in the basement of a well-worn building in town, which still had ashtrays above the urinals in the circa 1970 bathrooms.

An impressive figure, he was over six feet tall, full head of his own black hair, a fit build, handsome, with a friendly demeanor and firm handshake. That day he was wearing a light pink shirt with a matching tie, black slacks and open-toe slippers with white socks, taking the edge off what may have been an intimidating first encounter.

"Hello Dr. Linchitz, nice to meet you," I said.

"Hi, please call me Rick."

And with those simple greetings, began a friendship that lasted ten years and transformed my life on many levels.

The Wrong Man for the Job

Till that moment, I was not sure that marketing holistic, concierge or integrative doctors was the kind of work I wanted to do. It was more a hobby for me that I did because it seemed fun. And really, I did not know what the work was (or how to approach it) even if I did want to take it more seriously.

My partner and I ran a company that brought Ph.D. Psychologists into medical centers around New York to test and treat PTSD in people who were injured in work- and auto-related accidents. It was profitable, insurance-based, and . . . I hated it. I was bored out of my mind and strongly disliked the bureaucracy. During the first two years of this endeavor, however, I met many of the doctors who inspired me with their passion and commitment for helping their patients and who also had a complete disregard for the business part of their practice. Paradoxically, many of the amazing doctors I met were struggling financially because they did not know how to play the insurance game or simply did not want to. They were the very definition of a "starving artist", choosing to do what is best for the patient practicality be dammed.

So I started a radio program that would highlight some of these doctors and share their life-altering philosophy with the public. It was a paid program, where I purchased 30 minutes once a week on one of the oldest radio stations in the country and interviewed my guests (mostly chiropractors at the time) about their view of health and healing. After a year, I received the equivalent of a Master's Degree in Wellness, based on the philosophy of BJ Palmer—the founder of Chiropractic, 'the profession', he said, 'that worked with the subtle substance of the soul, release the prisoned impulses that tiny rivulet of life that emanates in the mind, flows over the nerves to the cells and stirs them to life.' The kind of things I learned were so common sense, so easy to understand and so completely buried under layers of misinformation and propaganda that were altering my view of reality. It was fun, educational and exhilarating.

Many of my guests said many of the same things: "The power that made the body heals the body . . . Health comes from the inside out and not inside in . . . Drugs don't cure anything but simply cover up symptoms of an underlying problem . . . Exercise is not simply for looking fit, it is crucial for staying well . . . The food you choose to eat directly interacts with your genetics and either activates or deactivates inherited diseases in the DNA from generations past." And of course, when I interviewed Jack LaLanne, the iconic fitness guru, it was: "If it tastes good, spit it out."

Over the ten years of the radio program, I interviewed many hundreds of doctors, bestselling authors, policy experts and celebrities who spoke about health, fitness, nutrition or the reversal of chronic disease by addressing the underlying cause of either the body having too much of what it does not need or the lack of something it does.

I knew that this was something I wanted to dedicate my life to, if only I could figure out how to make a living at it. I guess that I am, too, an impractical artist at heart.

You Can't Sell What You Did Not Buy

Interestingly, up until that point in my life, I had never been really sick although in my ignorant early years I ran myself pretty hard. Having started when I was 15, by the time I was 23, I smoked 3 packs of the red Marlboros per day. My favorite daily meal came from a sausage cart on the corner of 47th and 11th avenues ran by a heavily-mustached vendor by the name of Mohammed. I drank mostly soda and hardly any water. Since we painted yellow cabs in the shop where I was spending most of my days, when I got home it took some effort to wash all the yellow dust that was settled around my nostrils and hair, as well as the grease off my hands. Since the morning shift (when the night drivers handed off their cabs to the day drivers) was at 5 am and the evening one was at 5 pm (reversing the handoff), I worked very long hours and, one time, (when I was 16) it was 36 straight. I remember clearly trying to stay awake on the drive home after one of the biggest snow storms of the year. I had the heater on as I drove down the abandoned Grand Central parkway from the west side of Manhattan to Queens with piles of snow on either side of the wide road. As I began to drift to sleep (and the car started to coast from the far left lane all the way to the service road on the right at some 75 mph), it was a miracle that I opened my eyes just in time to avert disaster. I stopped the car a bit too abruptly, my heart pounding in my ears and the adrenaline pulsating through my body. I opened both windows, turned off the heat and (at 30 mph) continued the drive home.

So it's a bit coincidental (or some may say divine) that I only started developing chronic health symptoms about a year after I began my radio show promoting holistic doctors. At first, it was some flaky skin just above my right ear. Since I've never seen a doctor in my adult years, I just did what I usually do; I ignored it. Later, I bought some cream with aloe and used it to soothe the skin. But as it continued getting worse, I reluctantly decided to go see a dermatologist. At the time, we had one of the best health insurance options through my wife's job, so I called to make an appointment with one of the doctors in the network. I got an appointment two months from the day I made it. Finally, when the day arrived, I showed up at the doctor's office about 15 minutes before my scheduled time, filled out all the paperwork the front desk staff asked me to fill out, and I sat and waited.

It was over an hour later that I was finally invited into one of the exam rooms where I waited for another fifteen or so minutes, reading all the brochures depicting pictures of frightened people with advanced cases of a similar skin condition; and trying to chat-up the anatomically perfect skeleton, who was probably also waiting for the same doctor.

Finally, a man in a white coat walked through the door, holding a file. He introduced himself, asked what brought me to see him, and after examining the inflamed, flaky skin above my ear, wrote out a prescription for a steroid cream as he gave me a one word diagnosis. Psoriasis. And three minutes later, Elvis left the building, leaving me (script in my hand) and the other very patient patient looking at each other wondering what just happened.

Over the next couple of weeks, as I applied the cream to my skin, it would clear virtually overnight. Very nice. Except that a few days later it would come back and cover even more area of my scalp. So I put more cream. Now I had a new spot on the bottom of my left leg, just above the ankle. But on top of that, my joints began to hurt and, likewise, my wrists, fingers and (worst of all) hips, making it progressively difficult to walk or get up from a chair. Later, it was diagnosed as Psoriatic Arthritis, a chronic, auto-immune disease with no known cure in the world of allopathic, evidence-based care. So all of sudden (like the many doctors who became integrative healers because of a personal health struggle) for me, as well, the game changed.

Foundation: The Most Important Part of Any Structure

The symbolic cornerstone of the Freedom Tower was laid on the 4th of July in 2004. Between laying the actual foundation and all the details necessary for its completion, the finished work took almost four years. Once the most complex and important part was finished and the cranes were brought in, it took another four years to complete the rest of the 104 floors and have the building ready for occupancy. That is remarkable when you think about it. It took almost as much time and expense to build the part that no one will really see, or appreciate, as it did the 1776 foot structure that can be seen glistening in the sun from miles away.

We began slowly, Rick and I. For the first two years of working together, I interviewed him on our radio show. He spoke and exhibited at events that we created, and (every few weeks) we would sit down and discuss our progress and his evolving view of what he wanted to do with his newfound mission. At first it was integrative care. People with chronic conditions would come to him frustrated with the standard care of insurance-based allopathic doctors who did not have the time (or training) to identify the underlying cause and would simply prescribe another medication that would suppress symptoms and do nothing to actually resolve the problem. As Rick once described it, it's like trying to solve an overflowing sink problem by coming up with every conceivable way to vacuum the cascading water off the floor, not giving a thought about either turning off the faucet or clearing the blockage from the drain.

Working with Rick as my doctor, he quickly identified the underlying cause of my health issues through numerous testing protocols. And then using nutrition, supplementation, exercise, detoxification and stress management, it took about three months to permanently reverse the arthritic symptoms and significantly reduce the inflammation in the skin.

So now I'm a believer.

The Six Pillars of Vibrant Health

It did not take a long time for me develop a fondness for Rick that was something resembling brotherly love. He was kind, funny, tenacious, generous, brilliant, humble, and he was good to his word. When Rick agreed to something there was no reason to second guess, you could pretty much count on it. He had a philosophy that would not permit circumstances to affect what he said he would do, and so the universe would bend around his word, rather than the other way around.

I was sitting at a red light, playing with the stations of the car radio, when my phone rang. It was Rick. "Alex, do you have a minute?" he asked. "Sure. What's happening?!" I asked cheerfully, with a slight emphasis on the "*ha*", of *ha*ppening. He began to explain that his cancer progressed to stage four; he was using an oxygen tank to breathe and was in constant and severe pain. With the expo just a month away and the marketing out full force, he was concerned of not being physically able to speak at his scheduled lecture.

At that point, what could I say?

I was heartbroken on so many different levels; it was difficult to maintain a professional demeanor. "I'm sorry," was all I could muster as my voice began to crack. I just never gave it any thought. I never considered the possibility that his cancer was anything but conquered; this news came at me so unexpectedly that it shocked me to a deep personal loss, one that is still with me, although in a different form.

The day of the expo came fast, as it always does. I resolved myself to having to make concessions and breaking the news to those people who will be sitting in his lecture room waiting for a speaker who will not be there because he is dying. Except—to my surprise—Rick showed up. He came early and stayed the entire day, taking a few incognito breaks to breathe some oxygen from a portable tank. He spent the day speaking to as many people as he could and gave of himself as generously as ever. Before I introduced him to a standing-room-only crowd of hundreds, I gave him a hug, even though he was never very comfortable with that, and I knew it. "Ladies and gentleman," I paused. "It is my great pleasure to introduce to you, my doctor, my mentor and my friend . . . Dr. Richard Linchitz."

At that point I had to leave the room because the tears welled up in my eyes, and my soul was both inspired and torn. In the face of such pain and discomfort, this remarkable man still chose to do what he said he would. I'm not sure what drove that kind of honor and grace, but it was more saintly than human. It was the essence of the divine. It was also quintessential . . . Rick.

It's Eerily Quiet Before Blast Off

Rick was intimately involved in the development of the marketing I did for him. He was open to my opinion since he spent the majority of his time thinking about healing people, and I, about flyer design and other such sundry nuances of marketing and promotion.

At first, the response trickled in. There were a dozen people at his early lectures, and a patient or two would find their way to Rick's office and reference Health Media or the *Nutrition, Aesthetics, Vitality, Efficacy, Life* (NAVEL) expo (an event that grew to attract many thousands of health-conscious people) as to how they learned about him. The growth was slow and steady. Lecture attendance grew from one event to the next and soon his lectures were being filled to capacity with those who learned about him from our marketing efforts. More importantly, referrals came from those who experienced his unique approach to healing and told their friends to come listen to what he had to say.

Once we broke through the inertia and momentum grew, his lectures were filled to capacity and word-of-mouth spread like wildfire. Still, at the time, it was an uphill battle. Holistic doctors (who would routinely spend an hour or two with a patient, trying to identify the underlying cause) were not able to accept insurance for their services, primarily because it was the structures of insurance-based paradigm that did not permit the doctor to practice this kind of personalized medicine. That fact (and the extensive additional training necessary) made his services all out-of-pocket, relatively expensive, and mostly unaffordable for many who wanted it.

At the same time, we were competing with the government—one who pays doctors with a seemingly similar medical degree to see patients who don't have to pay anything themselves. So it was very difficult to sell the idea of fee-for-service medicine, an approach where our doctors spend all the time necessary to identify what is causing your symptoms and aim to resolve them permanently, if you believe that all medical care should be free. And when you can go across the street and see a doctor for $10 bucks and a flash of your insurance card, it becomes even more confusing for people. Sure, he will spend three minutes with you before handing you a prescription for some symptom-suppressing drug, but at least it's free. Although most times, if you've spent any time on this planet, you know that even if you got something for nothing, you got nothing, and gave up everything. Another way of saying it is that there ain't no free lunch.

A Penny for Your Thoughts

If I offered you $10,000 in cash right now or a brand new shiny copper penny, which would you choose? Did I hear you make a face?! Sure. The answer to that silly exercise is fairly simple. But what if I promise to double your penny tomorrow and every day after for the next 30 days? Which would you choose then?

It's a fun law known as geometric compounding. Most people would choose the $10,000 and they would be smart to do it. Take the cash, put it in your pocket, bring it home to your wife and all kind of nice things happen. But tell her that you have two more pennies that you have to drive over and pick up tomorrow, and nobody needs that kind of ugly. How many of us can walk around with a handful of magic beans in our clinched fist, believing that they are the answer to our prayers and the doorway to a new kind of life we've always dreamed. And do that for years on end.

As the penny continues to double, after 15 days you'll have $163.84, and everyone is telling you how you made the dumbest mistake of your life. Forget about this pipe dream and go get a job like all the other grown-ups, they preach indignantly. They continue to give you really good advice that you just refuse to listen to, but there you are with hardly any money, your wife has to get a job, her family thinks you're a deadbeat and now it's really beginning to eat away at your enthusiasm, confidence, and in turn, your work ethic. Maybe they are right, you start thinking. Maybe I should just drop this craziness, get a real job, and start earning a living you whisper to the deflated reflection in the bathroom mirror. So you find yourself between a rock and a Glock, stepping both on the gas and the break at the same time and with similar force. You start moving more cautiously, much more mechanical, doubting your every decision, fearing every tenuous step. And finally, if you are like most, you succumb to the pressure and give up. You shut the gates, close the door, and turn off your dream.

Thankfully, you and I are not like most. You and I are different than most. We are made out of the same cloth, weaved out of the same DNA as the likes of Richard Branson, Oprah Winfrey, Bill Gates and Henry Ford, with a bit of Winston Churchill thrown in for good measure. Sure, maybe we don't make as much money as they or wield the same amount of power and influence, but neither did they when they were us.

But can you imagine that one day you are going to create something as magnificent with your life as those legends did with theirs? What if your great, big, audacious dream will actually come to fruition? What if the thing you're doing now will be the next big thing tomorrow? And finally, what if it was already true? How would your attitude be different today, if you could go 10 or 20 years into the future and see how your dream came together? How would you deal with setbacks, rejection, and insults as well as ignorant negativity from those around you right now? What if you were that certain? How would knowing that your success is inevitable affect your confidence in the moment? How much quicker could you get to the realization of your vision if you already saw the Promised Land; a land overflowing with milk and money, and freedom? How would your conviction of tomorrow's success change your attitude in this moment of struggle?

On day 20, after all the work and effort, after spending all of your available resources on marketing, promotion and salaries, your doubling penny produced $5,242.88. Just over 50% of what you could have easily had in cash three weeks ago, if you weren't so darn stubborn.

But really, I am very happy that you and I did not give up or choose the road most traveled; that we did not take the same exit—one paved with concrete and lined on each side with interlocking barriers, leading everyone who takes it to the same pool of mediocrity. I'm glad we saw that vision no one else did and we fashioned it as a sculptor who chisels away everything extra to find his own unique David inside the block of shapeless marble.

On day 21, at $10,485.76, you surpass the original cash option and, at day 25, you hit $167,772.16 where finally you can start paying off some of the debt you accumulated over the years up till this point. And now is when it gets mind-blowingly fun. You are not working any harder. You are not any smarter or charismatic. You are the same guy (or if you wear a dress, gal) as you were when you only had that shiny penny and the scorn of almost everyone around you. Now (at day 30) you grossed $5,368,709.12 and, at the same time, you are referred to as an entrepreneurial genius, with the accolades of support and encouragement from everyone around you overflowing.

You are absolutely the same, but throughout this experience, your dream (which was some nebulous and invisible idea in your mind) finally manifests itself in a tangible form and can be seen, felt and experienced by others. Now it's real, and you have been validated. But you also know that you do not need validation now, and really, you did not need it when you had but your shiny penny in your hand and a hint of a dream in your mind, either.

Full Throttle Prepare for Takeoff

We were sitting in the spacious office of the 5,000 square foot space that Linchitz Medical Wellness recently moved in to. It used to belong to Acclaim Entertainment an international electronic game company that brought us games like *Iron & Blood: Warriors of Ravenloft*, so believe me when I say that no expense was spared for the decoration, furniture or design of the space. The carpeting was plush, the paneling oak. There were fireplaces in each room and the window shades worked by remote. Rick was thinking big, primarily because he never thought small, and although he did not mention it back then, time was of the essence.

It took about two years from the time Rick began in his tiny basement office until the moving truck pulled in front of one of the most prestigious buildings in town. It was definitely a stretch, but one based on the practical experience and confidence of knowing he could pull it off. It was also motivating and inspirational, bold and courageous. The mistake most people make is they start with an office and overhead that they cannot afford when they first begin. It's the equivalent of heading down the runway in a full-to-capacity tractor trailer, hoping it will take flight before you run out of asphalt.

It was then, sitting in that new office that Rick decided to put the throttle, on his integrative medical office version of the Jet Falcon 900, all the way down. Whatever experience he and I gained in the two years of working together in an industry that was new to both of us, we were ready and eager to take the game to a new level. And that is exactly what we did. At the time, it was still just him in that large and intimidating new space, but he was confident it would work out, and I was determined to help.

We positioned Rick next to well-established names in the field of integrative care and Anti-Aging; everyone from Suzanne Somers, Bernie Siegel, Gary Null, Carol Alt and Mark Hyman to name a few, all of whom spoke at our live events. We created a newsletter that was insert-mailed to over 750,000 homes prior to each event, reaching over two million people. We wrote an article-ad expressing the personal experience of one of Rick's patients (who happened to be me), placed it in a publication we created and, using a street team, distributed as many as 30,000 copies prior to each event. We made post event videos and recorded the lectures. We placed Rick as a spokes-person throughout our media partners. He was interviewed on national radio programs, magazines and television stations. We brought writers, photographers and video people to create the tools to better place Rick and his message in front of as many of the right kind of people as possible.

It was exciting, consistent and fun, but it was also kind of like running in the dark and (because we did not really know how to do it exactly) it worked really well, primarily because there was virtually nothing that I wasn't willing to try, and similarly Rick (for the most part) was only happy to let me do.

I once had an idea for a promotional photo where I would dress up in an Uncle Sam outfit, representing the American people, and Rick and his staff would all gather around me checking my vitals, representing the team that transforms the health of the nation. Then I would take a few photos in my red, white and blue speedos, in the evolution-of-man pose, for the before and after shots of my transformation. When I presented the idea, Rick did not bat an eye. 'Great, let's do it.' It was pure magic.

You Are Free to Move About the Cabin

Within a couple of years after that 'pedal to the metal' meeting, Rick's office was thriving. He had 19 professionals working, as he personally focused his attention exclusively on those patients battling cancer, and was booked for months ahead. His private label vitamin business, run by his son Jon, was developing its own impressive presence and was fast becoming a substantial part of the practice.

Once, when I came in to see Rick during his lunch break, his desk was covered with sticky notes of calls he needed to return. So he was eating his lunch, talking to me and fielding calls at the same time; it was brutal. I shared my concern about his break-neck schedule, but he just smiled. It was just who he was; it was the way he did life, just like a perpetual triathlon. It's both what made him great and what may, in all probability, have undermined his health.

When I share this story of the rags-to-riches success of Linchitz Medical Wellness with people, they usually ask if I feel that it was the marketing I did that helped Rick grow his practice so effectively. "It didn't hurt", is my usual answer. Rick was an amazing person and a remarkable doctor, who believed in his work passionately and looked the part of the integrative, Anti-Aging doctor, primarily because he himself did not seem to age or gain an ounce of fat on his lean, sculpted frame. Really, selling Rick was kind of like marketing the iPhone; all I needed to do was let people know what it did and that it was available. From that point on it kind of sold itself, and people lined up around the block to get it.

Today, I am in the unique position of having over 10 years' experience, primarily marketing integrative doctors and companies that create healthy living technologies and services. In a word, rebels. I've learned so much through the process of trial and error and error and error, and have seen very smart people make similar rookie mistakes over and over again. It pains me when I see it, and to the best of my ability, I try to communicate that although the earth looks flat and all of our senses tell us that the sun revolves around this Frisbee-looking planet, it is (in actuality) very different. And although knowing the truth may set you free, trying to sell it may get you burned at the stake. Similarly, if someone is determined to fail, it will take an act of G-d (or congress) to change it, so at this point, I no longer try. Simply, I look for people who want to succeed, have a passion for their work, are the embodiment of the message they are trying to communicate, and then I help them do it. That's fun.

Sponsors and Strategic Partnerships

After working together for a few years, Rick's practice was continuing its precipitous climb, and Health Media remained its main source of marketing, although at this point they were inundated with marketing and advertising opportunities. One day I came into his office for our meeting and suggested that there are service companies that are reaping substantial benefits from working with Linchitz Medical. After spending a small fortune getting this center off the ground, I pointed out that, perhaps, we should invite some of those companies to offset a portion of the marketing expense.

Most of the companies who work with doctors' offices do extremely well; from labs and Compounding Pharmacies to MRI's and supplement manufacturers, but (for the most part) they will never invite themselves to support the business responsible for much of that success. It's kind of like going to lunch with someone who conveniently goes to wash their hands when the check arrives. This "bowing out" happens because there are well-lobbied and confusing legal and ethical lines that make health care a complex terrain to navigate. But really, it's because most service companies are looking out for number one. They will spend all kinds of money to position themselves in front of the doctor to sell their services to them. But to get them involved in supporting the doctor in the marketing and promotional efforts of their center is an uphill battle.

I spoke with a doctor who recently opened his own practice in this integrative space. He was indignant that many of the companies (who he gave so much business to for many years prior when he worked for an established center) made no offer to help. It is interesting how many preconceived notions we have when we stumble into the strange and wonderful Avatar-like world of self-employment. We think things should go a certain way or people will behave how we think we would; but one thing is certain, the best way to start a new enterprise is to keep your assumptions on a short leash, less you be disappointed or fall off the edge of the earth into a fiery abyss. And worse, waste a whole lot of time waiting for things to happen that never will.

It is crucial then, to have the flexibility to shift your view and attitude as soon as you realize that you can't really walk on water (even though you were certain you could) and start doggy paddling as if your life depends on it, immediately after you figure that out.

Speaking to service organizations from a position of power will most usually produce results. It did not take a long time for some of the companies that serviced Rick's office to begin making substantial contributions to Health Media, so as to help us place Rick in front of more of his potential patients, grow the market share for the center, as well as for all of the businesses that benefited from his success.

Should this new office attempt the same thing, I would be surprised if anyone would give them the time of day. It's one thing to say, "Hey, we give you guys a ton of business. You should probably be involved in the process a little bit." And another when you lament, "Hey, we're just getting started. Please help us." One is operating from a position of power, the other from false assumptions and pre-conceived notions. It almost seems unfair; people are willing to help you when you're prospering and no longer need it, and won't return your calls when you're fighting for survival.

As some of the mourners who attended the funeral that *day began to ceremoniously throw a shovel of dirt on the simple wooden coffin, it began to drizzle. Moments later, someone screamed as people started pointing to the sky. There was a round rainbow circling the sun that was straight above our heads.*

In Rick's final days, Rita (his wife of over 30 years) asked that once he crossed over he give her a sign that he was ok. Throughout his life, Rick was responsible for many miracles; I imagine that this was just one more.

Atlantis: The Lost Center

A year later, I was once again sitting in that same office where Rick and I met and decided to put the pedal to the metal not so long ago. The new owner bought the practice shortly before Rick's passing and took a completely different approach to marketing it. They hired a consultant who placed ads in all the magazines throughout Long Island, paying premium price with little to show for it. They paid experts for web optimization, rebuilt the website, placed ads on the radio and television and engaged social media.

When they finally asked to speak with me, the practice had mostly deteriorated to the point of no return. They still had a fine staff, brilliant doctors and all of the infrastructure for a successful integrative center, but something had drastically changed and it had detrimental effect on the health of the enterprise.

Trying to defibrillate the center and get it moving in the right direction, I agreed to once again get involved although they were only willing to provide half the resources of years prior because the center was in a figurative nosedive. It was heart-breaking to watch; practical business men (who had no idea about the ethos that made this place work) came into an enterprise built by the soul and passion of a man with a vision began to wrap their clammy hands around the neck of this beautiful goose and try to choke the golden eggs out of it.

This was an emotional endeavor for me. I would have loved to see the practice miraculously come back to life and continue the legacy of my friend for many years to come so I dove in with everything I had. Taking the owner's word on the agreement, I prominently positioned all of their doctors in the marketing prior to our next event and then at the event itself. My team and I worked diligently, promoting our speakers and exhibitors through all possible venues, leveraging media and publicity, and stretching our marketing budget till it screamed for mercy. This exhaustive effort resulted in the best attended event we have ever produced with generous praise and accolades from our speakers and exhibitors.

A couple of weeks prior to our event, we reached out to the office letting them know that we still had not received payment for an invoice we sent months ago. We were told, "The check is in the mail." A few days later we called again, and were promised payment the following week. And after the weekend of the event, they no longer returned our calls.

As hard as we tried to pull this falling plane out of a nosedive, we failed. Soon after, their top doctors left the practice and all of the well-trained supporting staff went their own way as well. Whatever it was that made that office work could not be duplicated by men who neither had soul, vision or integrity.

Interestingly, sitting in that office with the new owner, every fiber of my being was screaming not to get involved. I did anyway and, even though I lost, I have no regrets.

Rick, this one is for you.

Something to think about: *My word is not a sail driven by the winds of circumstance; it is the stone on which they break.*

Chapter 3

Jigsaw Selling

"Business has only two functions — marketing and innovation." — *Peter F. Drucker*

When my son was as young as three, very adorable years old, he loved puzzles. At first, they were fairly simple; a jigsaw made of four pieces and then, as he got better at it, the puzzles grew in size and complexity. Eventually, they were a thousand tiny pieces of some elaborate landscape that were occupying his time, challenging his mind and taking over the dining room table.

Over the last thirty years, as an entrepreneur with an emphasis on marketing, my puzzles of how to deliver a message to its rightful owner and motivate them to action, grew in a similar fashion. I began by printing and distributing flyers and placing them under the windshield wipers of what seemed like a million cars throughout the West Village of Manhattan, back when I was selling oil changes and tune ups.

Today, there are many more gears that operate this multifaceted machine we call Health Media Group, an enterprise singularly focused on marketing integrative doctors and optimal-health supporting companies. We've painstakingly built this platform over the last ten years, using everything from newspaper and magazine ads, speaking at events and organizations, publishing our own periodicals, using mobile billboards and stationary road signs, television, radio, publicity stunts, media partnerships, telephone-marketing and giveaways, public relations, social media, YouTube and Google ads, as well as the live events we organize attracting thousands of people from around the world; all with the goal of creating the most fertile environment for the growth of the greatest of all marketing platforms—that elusive and coveted word-of-mouth.

Marketing is not an exact science. It changes from one year to the next and, over the last decade, it can hardly be recognized. So our goal is to find the right combination of ingredients to make the perfect sauce for the individual person that we happen to be serving and are looking to promote. And that is something that takes time, thought and commitment from both the marketing company and its client.

In this chapter, I'd like to share the approaches that were successful and those that flopped, as well as the recipe for marketing the integrative physician and companies that support optimal health that we found to produce the best results. Many of the lessons we learned, and share here, can be applied to virtually any industry.

You Dug Through My Trash

I will do virtually anything to reach a prospective client with the message I believe will benefit them . . . short of digging through their garbage, that is; find a piece of bulk mail I sent them that they inevitably threw away, and then return it in an envelope asking them to please take another look? I simply would never do that, although many thought that was exactly what I did.

At the time, I was marketing psychologists who did testing and therapy with work-related and motor vehicle accident survivors into medical centers around New York. Mostly it was a 'who you know' kind of industry; the well-established guys were servicing the larger and busier offices, and generally there was no interest in some new guy that no one knew or trusted.

So if I was going to make any progress, I would need to start reaching out to as many of the smaller offices around New York as I could and begin making some headway there. So I went to one office. "No, thank you." I went to another. "We don't need that, thank you." Five more, ten . . . nothing.

So I started writing letters and mailed thousands of them in sequences of three, using our custom letterheads. The first was a simple letter of introduction. The second, a week later, explained briefly how I could help their office. The third had further explanation of benefits and an invitation for a brief call that I was happy to initiate. Finally, I began finding offices that were willing to speak with me and learn more. Many eventually became clients.

As I got creative with all this direct mail and was looking to better grab the attention of the busy doctor or office manager, I sent a 4 x 6 post card to about 1000 offices throughout the New York area briefly explaining our services. It was standard mail with permanent indicia for the stamp and an electronically printed address. Then about a week later, I took another 1000 identical cards, printed the same address contacts as the last time, crumpled them up and put each one in an envelope addressed to the person on the card. The enclosed letter said something to the effect of: you accidentally threw out this very important piece of information and we took the liberty of sending it back to you for another look.

That definitely got people's attention. It was just not the kind of attention I was looking for. There were dozens of irate calls and letters with some version of, "HOW DARE YOU DIG THROUGH MY GARBAGE", and something about a restraining order in the content. And although one doctor did call to say that he was impressed with the creativity of the campaign, I didn't get any business out of it. But at least I got to see what does not work with my prospects, learn from the mistake, and try something new.

My Doctor Is a Marketing Genius

The first doctor who actually wrote me a check to do this kind of marketing for him was an old time chiropractor in Ozone Park, by the name of Robert Matrisciano. Dr. Matrisciano, (as I always called him respectfully, and never the less formal *Robert)* was just a few years away from retirement when I met him. Very distinguished, he had a well-groomed head of silver hair, a quick smile and always dressed well. He was in good physical shape, and although an injury he sustained in the service damaged both of his knees and made it painful to walk, you would never tell just by looking at him. He was a Green Beret during the Korean War and once shot and killed a mugger who attacked him one night as he was closing the office. A tough, brilliant man who was, seemingly, not afraid of anything or anyone and had a way of looking at things that I found fascinating.

He and I quickly became friends and he would encourage my ideas to promote his center and the Chiropractic profession as he took the time to share his philosophy about life, business, politics and healing. By that time in his career, Dr. Matrisciano really did not need the money, the exposure, or the few extra patients I brought to his center, but I think he saw in me someone who believed in his methodology and could, perhaps, help spread his ideas of natural approaches to health and life.

At one time, Dr. Matrisciano was also one of the most successful chiropractors in the country. His practice was all cash. He accepted no third-party reimbursement of any kind and, at this point, he was treating third generation patients who were willing to drive from hours away to see him. He did so well that he purchased the building where he had his office shortly after he began, paid top dollar to two full time secretaries who worked with him for 30 years, and drove a Rolls Royce. Even after he sold his building and retired, there were still so many who depended on him that he was forced to rent space in another doctor's office near his home so he could see patients once a week. And still they drove from all over the tri-state to see him.

I asked him several questions in our many, hour-long conversations, one of them being: How were you able to enjoy such success in an industry and profession fraught with failure? To answer my question, he used a story because, like that fella with long hair from Nazareth, Dr. Matrisciano also taught in parables.

When he first got started, chiropractic wasn't legal in the United States, and doctors like him were routinely arrested for practicing medicine without a license. But when you believe in what you are doing and you've experienced helping people get well, there was no way he was going to stop. "Besides, what can they possibly do to me that was worse than facing death in Korea," he asked rhetorically.

"I spent a lot of time promoting my center in those early days," explained Dr. Matrisciano. "I would cold-call people, send them letters, and once I had this idea where I picked up the local yellow pages and arbitrarily sent invoices to hundreds of the names listed. Many called back to dispute the bill and, after apologizing for the mix-up, it was my opportunity to talk to them, get to know them a little bit and tell them how I could help them with their health situations."

The Puppy Dog Close

In his bestselling book *How to Sell Anybody Anything*, author Joe Girard, who was inducted into the *Guinness Book of World Records* for the most number of cars sold to individual buyers in a single year, shares the story of how to use a puppy to close the sale. When a family comes in to discuss buying a car, Joe would hand the children a puppy to play with. As the negotiations continued and they were getting close to making a decision but just could not pull the trigger, Joe would say nonchalantly, "Hey, kids . . . if your parents buy the car today, you can have the puppy as a gift."

Clearly, neither of these examples would probably work today and you would most likely be frowned upon by your ethics professor, but one has to admire the audaciousness of the effort, both of these men were driven to accomplish a goal; they were willing to do virtually anything to get there. In other words, they put the pedal to the metal and only let up when they got to where they wanted to go. On the other side of the courage spectrum, I see a cautious, half-hearted, second-thought-effort to generate new business. Mostly it is because of fear, primarily covered up with the, 'I'm a professional and not a promoter', excuse. So otherwise brilliant people will put a nickel into a vending machine and stand there and wait for it to dispense a cold and refreshing bottle of Mountain Valley Spring Water that costs seventy five cents. Why not err on the side of results by putting a dollar bill in there, get what you want, grab the change and move on with your life? It's a much faster (and less frustrating) approach.

There Is a Leak in My Fuel Tank

The second car I owned as a teenager was a 1971 two-seat convertible Triumph TR6. Two guys pushed it over to my dad's taxi shop at 602 West 47th Street sometime during the summer of 1986. They did not have any money to fix it and wanted $125 dollars for us to take it off their hands. It was not in terrific shape. The original green color was faded, the back fender fins were rusted and missing, the interior paneling and soft top were missing and the engine needed rebuilding and the transmission replacing. It took me the next two years and a few thousand dollars to rebuild that car. Well, not really "me". It was nice that we had an auto-repair shop and, during slow times, I would ask the mechanics and the body men to help restore it. Once it was done, it really looked like it just came out of the dealer. Painted bright red, with a new black interior, soft top, wood grain dash and shifter knob, it was perfect; all the way down to the Union Jack flag stickers near the back stop lights.

It was that car I was driving back from upstate New York with my girlfriend one summer evening when I stopped at the gas station and asked the attendant to fill 'er up. As we continued driving home, I started hearing a noise near the back wheel. It grew more pronounced followed by the distinct smell of gas. And as soon as we passed the toll of the Tappan Zee Bridge, I pulled over to the side and looked under the car. The two round plates uniting the right axle were barely held together by just one of the four bolts that were originally there. As the axle opened up, it cut a gash in the fuel tank that was now leaking onto the exhaust, making a sizzle sound similar to water dripping on a hot skillet.

I found some tools and replacement bolts in a tool box I carried in the trunk, slid under the car and began fixing the axle as the warm gasoline poured down my arms and all around me with the strong fumes making a permanent impression on my senses.

There are two lessons that I took away from that experience. First, since I lived to tell the tale, luck can sometimes supersede stooopid. And second, business development is kind of like driving with a leaky fuel tank. If you are not constantly replenishing it, it is only a question of time till your business stalls on the side of some lonely highway.

Okay, maybe it's not the best analogy, but the bottom line is business never stands still. You can't just coast. As time goes on, things change and your best customers may no longer need you, so you start scrambling and thinking about marketing when you get a notice that the client you thought will always be there is not renewing. But then it's already too late . . . kind of like closing the barn door after your wife runs away on the back of your favorite horse with the guy responsible for keeping the barn door closed.

Can You See Me Now?

I recently started working with a doctor who is one of the top experts in the world in a particular modality that helps people structurally correct their eyesight and was able to help with some common problems for which mainstream medicine had no answers. He was servicing the Hasidim community and was getting a steady flow of referrals to his two offices. He was proud to say that he never had to advertise or promote himself even though he had built a multi-million dollar fee-for-service practice. The reason I found myself sitting in his office on this particular afternoon was because another doctor became a world expert in this same technique, and most of his patients left him and went there. Just like that. Overnight, and after some 30 years, his business ran out of fuel and there was not another station for miles.

Similarly, in one year, I lost my top four sponsors: one who passed away, the other who got a divorce and had to focus on her personal life, the third became a superstar and no longer needed my services, and the last stopped paying me and I had to let them go. That is the equivalent of that fuel tank leaking virtually dry, allowing me to get to the next exit mostly on fumes. But what then?

What Your Doctor Can Learn From My Shoe Shine Man

"Hey Mister, your shoes need shining!" – The man who had set up a shoe-shine stand on a New York street corner called to me as I was waiting to cross Sixth Avenue with my teenage daughter. I looked down at my feet and did not feel an immediate need to sit down on one of the two office chairs my innocuous accoster jury-rigged onto a wooden platform. "I'm good," I answered. Without skipping a beat, now focusing his smiling gaze at my 14-year-old daughter, "Miss, your boots need a shine!" One more time I looked down, now at the boots that were recently a prized possession of my wife. This time he hit the nail on the head. Those boots were in desperate need of exactly his kind of attention.

With a technique for shining shoes Don perfected over the last 20 years, he went to work with all the joy, speed and pride in his work of a true professional. As he was shining the boots, he continued making comments at the scruffy shoes of the people passing by, explaining the psychology of those who turned him down. "Those are trust babies. They did not like being called out on a perceived imperfection," he'd quip. At the same time, he shared his own surprising story with me.

"I was a pastry chef, then I lost my job and was jobless for over three years. Before that, I was an accountant working in a cubical. "Smiling at my daughter, he whispered as if sharing a secret, "That was boring. Don't do that!" Quickly returning to his story, he said "I had Johnny Carson in this chair; I told Ted Turner of CNN his shoes need shining. He did not have time for a shine but gave me a $20."

There are lots of things to love about Don; he is a free spirit, he did not settle for a government handout or a system that was, as he put it, referencing a Seinfeld episode 'killing independent George', he is a marketing machine, and he is good, very good at his work.

One of the things he said to me as I was standing there and waiting was: "There's no shortage of dirty shoes; you just have to figure out how to get them in the chair." So as he continued working on the customer he had in his chair at the moment, he never stopped making comments at the people passing by, and by the time he was finished and collected the $20 that I could not help but give him, there was already another customer standing there waiting to be enchanted, and her shoes shined.

Being on the defensive, with your fuel tank on empty and no one waiting to sit in your seat to have their proverbial shoes shined, makes it difficult to make tough decisions. If you have a problem client—one who sucks your time and life-energy and turns your business or practice into a collection agency because you are forced to chase them for a payment they should have made months ago—how can you possibly be effective in your main job? How can you, if you are being distracted by someone who isn't doing what they said they would, as they tinkle on your boots and tell you it's raining? And you can't let them go if you feel you need them and don't have many other options, hoping that maybe one day they will make good on their promise. But when your tank is full, you are constantly bringing in new clients and are able to pick and choose who you work with; I think that kind of environment fosters creativity, effectiveness, rapid growth and true success. Not to mention that it's just so much more fun that way.

A Line in the Sand

On the walls of my home office, there are pictures of me with many of the people who I met over the years; well-known faces of those who spoke at our events, as well as recognitions I received from the government, a signed letter from the president, the covers of magazines that we published, and a dated happy father's day poster from my daughter. At one point, I took everything down, leaving a large white board and the many picture-frame nails protruding from the peach-painted sheet rock. I decided to place the past where it belongs and, using a marker, a blank white board and a few brain storming sessions, create a future that inspires our best effort.

Certainly building on our past accomplishments is not a bad thing; looking back and gathering strength from our foundation can only be good, but if we live in the past, it also hampers our ability to create something from nothing. For that to happen, for us to tap our greatest strengths, creativity and motivation, we have to let go of the past (just like we only glance in the rearview mirror) and begin to create a future that we dream ourselves into. Then all of a sudden, we notice a door on that endless wall of opportunity; one that was always there but, somehow, we did not see and, as we push it open, we discover a world that is beyond our imagination and one we never knew existed.

Don't Touch That Dial!

Radio is a very powerful marketing tool. If you are able to get on a station that reaches a fairly large demographic, create your own talk show and stay on the air consistently, it is a good place to educate your listeners on the merits of your message and the benefits of your service.

It is an intimate platform where you are able to share your knowledge and build a relationship with those who tune in to hear you. You don't need to worry about what you are wearing or how you look, since the people listening create their own image of you in the confines of their mind. There are a few personalities on the radio that I really like and tune in to hear as often as my schedule permits. The people I enjoy most are smart on their topic, have an interesting take on the world, are passionate but not mean, and are very good at what they do. They also give generously of their knowledge and experience and genuinely have an interest in helping people (like me) who tune in to hear them. There are also some who I know personally and the only thing the radio did was amplify their arrogance and pompous self-aggradation times a thousand.

One doctor, in particular, has an hour-long show on a popular radio station in New York. Whenever anyone calls and begins explaining the health situation they are looking for some help with, his standard answer is, "Yes, we can help you with that. Call my office to schedule an appointment." Then he proceeds to give out the phone number. Clearly the only person he is out to help is himself.

It is a strange feeling, doing a radio program . . . much different than what one would expect. You kind of sit there in a studio that's the size of a walk-in closet. Maybe there is a producer behind the glass, maybe there is an in-studio guest, or perhaps you are on your own. There is a microphone in your face and some arbitrary pictures on the wall, but you are all alone speaking to an audience that you imagine in your mind. It's probably kind of like making love to someone invisible; it's still fun but, definitely, very strange.

Having your own show is the better option. Although you can also place ads that run throughout the day, in the former, people actually tune it to hear what you have to say. In the latter, you're trying to interrupt them and get their attention for about half a minute. One is a shovel, the other a bulldozer. Each is good for the job intended and are priced accordingly. If you are considering doing your own radio show, let me just caution you: it's expensive. Sometimes very expensive. You can easily pay $2500 per 30 minutes on a good-sized station. But really, if you've never done it before, starting at a smaller station is the wiser thing to do. Once you get comfortable, find some sponsors and develop a following. You have a much better chance of making it work. It's so much better than jumping behind the wheel of a 747, if you've never even flown a two-seat Cessna.

And it's time-consuming. Not only do you have to prepare for each show, you have to create the pre and post marketing for it, arrange guests and (if you are so inclined) read their books. It's tough for a busy professional to take the time to do that consistently, although I've met a few remarkable people who made it work successfully.

But Wait, There's More!

When I was running my auto repair shop, I read a terrific book by Chin-Ning Chu called *Thick Face Black Heart*. I got excited about the many lessons within like: *'character is not made of sunshine and roses. Like steel, it is forged in fire, between the hammer and the anvil'* and wanted to learn more. Somehow I found out that Chin-Ning was doing a conference in California, so I called to get some information. Surprisingly, she got on the phone herself, so I told her how much I liked the book and wanted to come to hear her speak. She asked me a few questions about what

I did and where I was from. This short call turned into an extended conversation and, after I gave her my contact information, we said goodbye.

About a week later, the beige rotary phone on my kitchen wall rang. It was Chin-Ning. She said "hello" and asked me if I wanted to be on CNN. "Excuse me, what?" I asked, although I heard her fine.

Turns out that the producers who were promoting her book were looking for a simple fella, not a corporate type but a Joe the Plumber kind-of-guy who can talk about how the book influenced his life. "Of course you do," she said assertively. "Okay, sure I'll do it," I answered. I think I was 25 at the time.

The crew arrived at my auto repair shop early in the morning; they miked' me for sound, turned on all the portable lights, aimed a huge camera in my face, and . . . *action*! It took about an hour of questioning about the book, my business, what I learned and how I think. It was over, and a star is born. Clients called me from all over the country to tell me they saw me on TV; one said he was in a hotel in Africa, and saw me there.

It definitely got me some attention and brought some accolades. Just no new clients. Not a one.

Getting media exposure is great but, many times, it creates a curiosity piece—one that gets a bit of attention and, maybe, builds a little street cred. But overall, I would not put all of my marketing eggs into that very cool, serendipitous (yet unpredictable) basket.

Alex Lubarsky

Money for Nothing and Your Ads for Free

Recently, I was contacted by a national publication that catered to some of the more affluent people in the country. It's pages discussed a dreamy lifestyle of mega homes, jewelry, yachts, exotic vacations, as well as cars that were not only meant to get you from point A to point B, but have everyone looking, pointing, and salivating (if only figuratively) as you make the trip. As more of their readers began to express interest in wellness and anti-aging, they were exploring the possibly of building a relationship with a media company focused on promoting it.

This was not the first time we had an opportunity to develop synergetic relationships with media companies. In the beginning, we partnered up with the largest Jazz station in New York City and, later, with a large news television station, and then numerous publications that were either in the wellness space or wanted to explore it.

So we were able to barter full page ads in national publications, air time on radio stations, promotions on television and other venues that offered many thousands of dollars-worth of media exposure. At the same time, we positioned our media partners at our events, and provided sponsor logo's and ads in our marketing materials. It is a terrific relationship because we place the media we work with in front of their public as those who are interested in helping their viewers become well, healthy and fit. At the same time, they have an opportunity to reach those who may not be familiar with them through our on-the-street, gorilla out-reach efforts.

So although I greatly appreciate these media people and their generosity in working with us, I try to allocate my advertising budget in their direction as well. So I've purchased ads on virtually every media company that we have that kind of relationship with.

Having said that, let me say this . . .

The Wisdom of the Ages

Many years ago, in a land far, far away, a great king wanted to collect the wisdom of the ages. So he sent his wise-men to the far reaches of his vast kingdom to collect it. Years later, as the much older and wiser men started to return, he gathered them and asked that they bring to him everything they learned. In short order, there were many volumes of thick, leather-bound books stacked from floor to ceiling overflowing with every kind of truth and law the world had to offer.

Standing in the center of this great library that now appeared before him, the king shook his head and said, "No one will ever read all of this." "Condense it and bring it to me in a way that the average person can read it and understand it," he commanded. A year passed by and they came back with ten much thinner volumes of the wisdom of the ages. "Still no good!" the king yelled. "No one is ever going to read all of that. Condense it further." So they came back with just one book. "Condense if further," the king repeated. They came back with one page. Still the king was not happy. A paragraph. Still NO. Finally, they came back with a sentence. And when the king looked at it, a knowing smile finally appeared on his face. He looked out on the sea of exhausted and pensive wise-men, and quietly read the words on the page in front of him: *There ain't no free lunch.*

So, yes, although I think it's important to leverage the value from media sources interested in doing an editorial about you, I also believe that it's a mistake to think you will build a media presence by trying to get it at will and for free.

When I had my radio program, for example, I would receive a daily pitch from a PR firm representing either a doctor, food bar company or personal trainer who wanted to get some publicity and thought simply sharing their blueberry smoothie recipe would get them on the air with a major news organization, or even a boutique one like mine.

Generally, the way I found my guests was to research and look for the kind of person that I thought would interest my listeners. Usually, they were bestselling authors, had a presence in the marketplace, were considered an expert on the topic, and also had a media persona that was comfortable in front of the mike or camera; or, they were one of the doctors who paid me to promote them. So if I ever chose someone the PR agency forwarded in an email blast addressed to no one, it would be very rare. And mine was a tiny, 30-minute radio show on a virtually unknown station in Nassau County, New York that was ethnic till 6 pm and had a relatively unimpressive reach.

Okay, now that we got that straight, *helpareporterout.com* is a place where you can get in front of some of the top media companies, and you can do it for free. It's definitely worth a shot.

How Bozzano Organic Olive Oil Can Save Your Practice

A couple of years ago, I was spending the weekend at one of the largest events on the planet, featuring everything organic, holistic and fantastic in the world of wellness and cutting-edge health. It is a professional event for those who are in the industry and attracts some sixty thousand integrative healers, health food store owners and the like. It features some three thousand exhibiting companies that sell high-end supplements, non-chemical beauty products and healthy food stuffs from organic coffee and protein bars to gelato and grass-fed beef.

I was there for four days, walking the floor of this massive city of healthy living, when I met Jack and Nancy Bozzano. They are the owners of a farm in California that grows organic olives and turns them into some of the finest, purest, high potency olive oil on the planet.

After a few minutes of conversation, it was easy to like this couple with their sincere, easy going manner. I was also impressed with their passion for producing high quality olive oil, as well as the fact that they are married for almost 50 years. As I took a sip from one of the little clear plastic sample cups, Jack explained that good oil will have a little bite in the back of your throat and that the higher regulation in California and the organic logo assures that it's 100% olive oil— one that, in lieu of chemicals, used a demanding, hands-on processes to manage bugs and the harvesting of the olive itself.

"And what is it that you do?" Jack finally asked.

"Well, I work with a network of wellness-oriented physicians in the New York area and in partnership with some of the media there, we produce events that attract thousands of people who have an interest in a lifestyle that fosters optimal well-being, lasting beauty, fabulous fitness and inspiring longevity. Then, I look for companies that I can introduce to our doctors and educate the public on the unique benefits of their product."

We shook hands, exchanged a farewell and a business card, and I continued my walk down the endless isles of people and products. It was a few weeks later that I called Jack, who surprisingly, remembered me right away. "You promised that you would make me famous," he said jokingly, quoting what I said as we parted last.

There are many people who have been cheering my efforts to bring wellness education to more people. One of the most consistent and amazing of them is Dr. Ellen Kamhi, who is a PhD, RN, a media personality and author of numerous books. So I asked Ellen if she would be open to being a spokesperson for Bozzano and educate people on the benefits of olive oil and how different oils affect our health. Even if she did not want to do it, I don't think Ellen could say "no" to me; so she readily agreed.

We had one of our writers interview Ellen and put together an article that we added to the magazine we use to promote the expo. She also had a lecture scheduled at our event a month after our publication came out. I asked my fifteen-year-old daughter to stand at the booth where we displayed the olive oil and, between the two of them, we quickly began moving the liquid health elixir like the proverbial hot cakes. After one of her lectures, people tripped over themselves to get to the booth and bought out all of those high end (and relatively expensive) bottles of some of the finest top-shelf, organic olive oil on the market. In addition, we had our street team drop off samples at some of the finest restaurants throughout New York, New Jersey and Connecticut as we promoted an upcoming event.

More importantly, this company and many like it, allow Health Media to leverage the marketing dollars of our doctors, more than doubling our purchasing power. Between that and our ability to barter with other media organizations, an integrative doctor can get what amounts to $10 worth of marketing for every $1 they invest with us.

If It's Good Enough for Elvis

If a product could be the embodiment of what we are trying to communicate to the public about our integrative doctors, if there was a way to have someone hold in their hand the quality, integrity, purity, attention to detail and unquestionable health benefits of integrative care, it is Mountain Valley Spring Water. I met Stuart Scott (the largest distributor of this bottled water) in New York, pretty much about the time I met Rick, at the very beginning of this endeavor. And like Rick, Stuart saw that there were obvious synergies between what his product had to offer and this wellness movement.

Since 1871, the Mountain Valley water company has been bottling this award-winning water in glass packaging. The water, itself, is sourced from a protected 2,000-acre reserve in Hot Springs, Arkansas. It has a high mineral content and is fairly alkaline at 7.8 pH. The health qualities of this water have been touted for many decades. Named the best water in the world, it was also the favorite water of some 15 US presidents . . . and Elvis.

Compared to other bottled water options that come in plastic, it is fairly expensive; but if you consider it's applications to communicate high quality and adherence to the very best for your patients as they see the water displayed in your waiting room, the value tremendously outweighs the cost.

The first time I saw this water it was in the office of Dr. Fred Jones, one of Long Island's most prominent chiropractic doctors. He had a five-gallon glass bottle and a dispenser in his waiting room. Most of the offices I've been to up until that point had a similar five-gallon plastic option; and when I learned of the potential health implications of BPA, a hormone-mimicking chemical in plastic that leaches into the water, it just made no sense to me to have that kind of message displayed in a healing center simply to save a few dollars.

So I bought a few cases of the Mountain Valley Spring Water one-liter bottles and began giving them out to everyone I met as gifts. Like the people who I market today, I really love this product and drink it myself almost exclusively. Since then, Stuart has become a good friend and a consistent sponsor of the wellness revolution and all of the leading players who drive it. We are very happy to march under the flag of this very embodiment of our healthy living message.

Something to think about: *Feed your business and it will build your lifestyle; feed your lifestyle and it will eat your business.*

Chapter 4

Can We Speak?

"It usually takes more than three weeks to prepare a good impromptu speech." – Mark Twain

The first time I ever spoke in public was when I was about 23 years old. I dealt with people all the time prior to that and was pretty confident (or perhaps, arrogant) when in my own circles, but nothing in my past could have prepared me for what was about to happen.

This particular day, I was invited to introduce myself to a room full of strangers who were all dressed in business suits and seated in a conference room of a hotel in Queens. So I came up to the front of the room, took the mike in my hand, moved it towards my face and (just after I said "Hi, my name is ...") lost all control of my body. My hands began to shake uncontrollably, my chest filled with tar, my mouth went dry, my legs buckled and my brain experienced a blackout. I was not expecting that, not even a little bit. I just thought I would go up there and speak to this group as I did one-on-one with a friend or two. It was kind of like sticking a hair pin into an electric socket, which seems like that's where it should go if you don't know better, and the result is always shockingly unexpected. That's kind of how I felt.

Everyone was very nice. The people in the audience felt for me and, after some pity applause, I finished, mercifully, found my way back to my seat and sat down. I was in shock and awe. What was that? I thought. How come I was not able to get my mind to work or put two words together? What was it about standing in front of a group of strangers that turned me into some version of a deer frozen by the oncoming headlights of a figurative semi-trailer?

After that experience, I learned that people feared public speaking more than death. Death, I say! I could see how that could be true though. Because after experiencing that much embarrassment, fear, loss of control, and the total evaporation of whatever little self-image I had squirreled away till that point, death seemed like a viable and compassionate option. So it's easy to understand why someone who experienced it once would never want to put themselves through it again.

True Freedom Is on the Other Side of Fear

After that experience, I knew that I had a speaking problem. There were only two choices for me. I could forget what I experienced, go back to my shop, lie down on a creeper and roll back under a car for the rest of my life; or I could jump out of the proverbial airplane and hope my parachute opens. So I joined the Dale Carnegie speaking course. It was an expensive investment for me at the time, but I knew if I was not willing to take that step at that moment, I probably never would.

It was an -eight-week program that allowed for a two-minute presentation in front of about 40 people at each meeting as they took you through all the success strategies of public speaking. With a focus on persuasive communication, interpersonal relationships, problem solving and becoming a focused leader, this was a revolutionary and enlightening experience. But having me in that class was just karma paying me back for what I, inadvertently, did to one of my mechanics not long before.

Martini came from the Dominican Republic when he was in his early 30's. He was a very hard working guy whose goal was to bring his family here to the US. He was a good mechanic, but his English was like many of the cars we saw—broken. As I began to get more serious about personal growth and continued to read books and attend different courses, I naturally wanted to help the people who worked with me grow as well. So I hired an English teacher who came into the shop every evening, and for a couple of hours, taught some of my staff how to talk in American. Then, I found a course that would help Martini become a better manager, because at the time, I was thinking of franchising my shop and have him run this one. So I sent him to a Nightingale Conant leadership course for managers and CEO's of small businesses held in Manhattan. It was primarily attended by some of the sharpest entrepreneurs in New York looking to hone their skills. He took the day off and spent most of it in this interactive workshop. The next day when he came to work, he just looked at me for a minute, shook his head and said, "Ale ju klecy." Well, yea I guess I'm a little crazy. But similarly in that environment of well-educated, well-dressed and well-spoken, 'human people', I felt like I was an alien from planet Stooopid.

After that initial training was done, I signed up as an assistant to the course leader. My job was mostly to set up the room, ring the timer and make sure the pens on the back table were laid out straight. But it allowed me to go through the course a couple of more times without having to pay for it, and at the same time, I became friends with the course leader, who helped me better understand the material and get a handle on being able to speak in front of a group.

SEC Roughriders Taught Me to Talk Good

Soon after I completed my final Dale Carnegie course, I joined one of the very best and oldest Toastmasters clubs in the country, the SEC Roughriders. Founded in 1956 by the titans of industry who wanted to improve their public speaking skills, it was held every Thursday at Noon in one of the wood-paneled offices of the NYC Bar Association building in midtown Manhattan. This club attracted some of the most dynamic speakers that I've ever seen. I spent months researching and visiting other clubs around New York, but this one was head and shoulders above the rest.

After paying my nominal membership dues, I received a manual in the mail with an outline for my first ten structured speeches, each focusing on a different skill as it regards speaking in public. One was for an icebreaker. It explained the protocols of how to deliver my first introductory talk and introduce myself to the group. Another was using a prop in your speech. Then it was enthusiasm, motivation, sales etc. Here, I had the opportunity to prepare a speech and then practice my speaking for six to ten minutes in front of a live audience of some 50 people about once a month. So, within a year, I completed the entire first manual and was ready to advance to the next level. The group was always kind and complementary, gently suggesting points for improvement and allowing me to grow through the process at my own pace.

About this time I became friendly with a fellow who was also a member in this club by the name of Billy Sparkle. He was about a head taller than I, with a thin build and a full head of thick, dirty-blond hair. And although he dressed well, his choice of shoes was a bit too "construction" for the suit and tie he always sported. His dream was to become a motivational speaker, business coach and author so he made the commute from Staten Island to midtown weekly to practice his craft. It was not uncommon for some of us to go out for a beer together, especially after a speaking contest where we would compete with other clubs around the city. And as our friendships grew, this club became a sort of extended family of friends, mentors and fans of each other.

After one of our weekly meetings, Billy and I went for some tea at a coffee shop around the corner on Sixth Avenue. "I am so frustrated," Bill said as soon as we sat down with our insulated paper cups in hand. "To get good at speaking in public, we have to do a lot of speaking in public, but no one wants to let us speak until we get good," he continued as he looked lamentably at the white lid of his hot drink. "I mean, I like this club, but at one speech per month that we are able to make there, it will take a lifetime before we can actually become comfortable enough to be considered professional and get over the fear that seemed like it was a body part that we'd never be rid of." Although it was he who was saying all this, it could just as easy have been me, because I felt the very same way. Raising his eyes to meet mine, he finally said, "I am at my wits' end. I'm actually thinking of just going down to the subway and speaking to the commuters riding the 'F' train."

I'll Never Speak in Public

Once a doctor called me and asked to take a booth at one of our events. I've heard of this physician before and had read a number of his articles published in a numerous magazines in our area. So I suggested he take a lecture slot to better communicate his message. That was the last I heard of him for two years. I later learned he had a serious phobia of public speaking. When we met sometime later, I told him that if he was looking to make the kind of impact he was hoping to make and if he really wanted to share his passion for his particular approach to healing, then he had to get over his fear of public speaking post-haste and turn that weakness into one of his greatest strengths. In a short while, this same doctor was nominated as one of the top speakers at one of our larger events by the thousands of people who attended. Sure, it was I who handed him the plaque, but it was the people in his lecture who were touched by his message and voted for him.

Yes, we can allow our fears to drive our decision process. We can justify and explain away why we won't do something we know we must, but ultimately, we are only lying to the man in the mirror. As it was said so many years ago:

"To thine own self be true, And it must follow, as the night the day thou canst not then be false to any man."— *William Shakespeare*

Excuse Me, Mister. Could You Spare Some Time?

I felt the cold steel of the vertical hand rail of the modern "F" train in my hand as we headed express from New York's 4th Street over the Manhattan Bridge to Brooklyn. A bead of sweat was rolling down my back as I stood there, frozen with fear, at the thought of actually saying something out loud. Billy was right next to me, looking just as terrified. We started at 42nd Street, and as the train continued its stops from one to the next, we were coming to the realization that this was not something either of us was going to do. To actually speak to the commuters on that train would have been simply insane. Sure, there are lots of panhandlers who do it (and people selling some version of their religion or those who peddle useless plastic noisemakers), but to bare your soul, to share your passion and do that on a NYC train car . . . that is just all kinds of crazy. So we just kind of looked at each other, defeated, as we planned to exit at the next stop and take the train back to where we started. Literally and figuratively.

"Hello Ladies and Gentleman. I know what you're thinking," I finally said out loud, startling myself and the 50 or so commuters who looked up from their newspapers to see what was happening. I was wearing a business suit, blue shirt, matching tie, and highly-polished, black shoes. This was not what these veteran commuters were expecting, so it took a moment for those seated to get the dichotomy of this situation. "This man is going to change my life," I continued jokingly. This was it; the beginning of our subway series of motivational speaking of sorts. It was how we began getting comfortable addressing a crowd of people we did not know, those who were not open to our message and (in some instances) were hostile to it. But that year, right up till September 11th 2001, we spoke on the train three times per week (three to five times each), some 500 two-minute talks over a period of a year.

As we discovered after some time, certain express trains traveled (from 42nd Street to 72nd Street, for example) without making any stops, and it would take two minutes or so, which allowed us to do our thing. We actually got pretty good at it, eventually printing round cards with the word "TUIT" in the middle. We would tell those people who were meant to be on our train, that if they had dreams burning in their soul, if they wanted to start a business, travel some place exotic or do something everyone thinks is crazy, *now* was the time to do it—not in some arbitrary future, or when they *get around to it*. And just in case, we would end our talk by handing out those round TUIT's we printed, explaining that now that they finally got it (a round TUIT), they could go out and live their dreams.

Most people were very generous and patient once they understood what we were doing and that we did not want anything from them other than just a couple of minutes of their time. Some offered us money (which we never accepted) and many emailed us encouraging messages to the address printed on the back of our round TUIT cards. Some followed us from car to car and shook our hands as they got off the train saying something to the effect of "thanks, I needed that". Of course, there were others who moved to the next car as soon as we came into the one they were in at the time.

You Are Not What You Think

One time, a woman began to shout "*shut up*" as soon as I began to speak. She looked like an average professional person traveling to work, but something set her off and she began shouting me down. I stopped speaking and let her vent, and as soon as she saw that everyone on the packed train-car was now staring at her, I explained that she was not being mean. She was not bad or wrong in any way; it was just her natural response to anyone doing anything that threatened her comfort zone set in place perhaps when she was just a child. In her mind, whenever she wanted to do something (or say something that was not in line with her perceived norm), "shut up" was what she heard. It was the default message permeating her thought process and limiting her experience of life. But once you understand that you are not what you think, you can change what you think and set yourself free. Sure you may have thoughts, yet *you are not your thoughts*. Like a record player is not the music of the record it's playing, so are you not the limiting thoughts that are currently playing in your mind and restricting your experience to a life you want, one that is lived in your dreams and on your terms.

One of my biggest fears, as we were going from one car to the next, was that I would see someone I know. That would be all kinds of embarrassing! If it was someone who was a friend, or maybe a relative, that would not be so bad; but if it was one of the people who I was working with currently, that would be very bad—devastating, in fact. So I never told anyone I was doing this. It was me and my friend Billy's little secret; like two suited crusaders for good, working to inspire Gotham, using our powers of the spoken word.

As I opened the door to the next train car (after Billy did his talk in the last) and made my quick introduction to get everyone's attention, a woman standing near one of the six sliding doors of this train car screamed out: "Alex!" And although her eyes were open wider than usual, I recognized her immediately.

"Susan!" I responded, trying to act nonchalant.

The company I was running at the time had over 20 PhD psychologists who I was marketing into centers around the New York area. Many also worked for prestigious institutions around Manhattan. Susan, a young and attractive doctor, was the first person I started working with and later became a managing partner of the group.

I was very embarrassed and did not know exactly how to proceed. At that moment, I was hoping that a great hole would open below my feet and swallow me up. Should I just talk to her and get off the next stop? Or should I finish the talk I started and explain myself later? After a quick "hello" and a few awkward moments, Billy encouraged me to finish my talk and give out our "round TUIT" cards. So I did, and when I was done, moments before the train pulled up to the next station, the people on the train began to applaud, with Susan leading the approving gesture.

The reason I am sharing all of this with you, is simply to say that it does not matter how we start out. What opportunities we are given or those we lack, each day we have a chance to break through our fears and doubts, stretch our abilities and take the kind of action that lays another brick in the structure that we will ultimately build with the moments of our life.

Infrastructure: How to Create Action Out of Mere Words

Over the years, I fell in love with reading and learning the fundamentals of a successful life. It did not take long to figure out that, although money is an important part of successful living, it is only a part. True success is having a passion for your mission, contributing and inspiring people around you, having the respect of your friends and the love of your family. At least the immediate family. So through books, I have collected many lessons about how to win friends and influence people, how to sell anybody anything, how to think and grow rich, how to see you at the top as well as the magic of thinking big and how to awaken the giant within. It is amazing that I can pick up a book by someone who spent a lifetime reading the lifetime experiences of other great people, as they accomplished their life's purpose, add their own ideas and allow me the privilege of gaining the benefits of all that experience and knowledge in a few evenings of reading.

One of the things I learned many years ago from a book called *How I Raised Myself From Failure to Success in Selling* by Frank Bettger, is the idea of setting up the upcoming week and planning exactly who you want to speak with and what you want to accomplish. Set aside your Saturday, he says, and spend six or so hours diligently planning your week, then be tenacious about accomplishing your blueprint and be very protective of your schedule. I thought it was a good idea; I just never could get myself to do it. Usually I would just start my day and try to hit all the pitches thrown in my direction (and maybe launch a few of my own). It has been a pretty good strategy until recently. Today, it takes me hours to check and answer my email, the messages on FB and Twitter. There are meetings to plan, hotels to book, and articles to write and approve. I am drowning in the nitty-gritty of my daily tasks, which leaves me no time to do things like prepare for a talk or get on the phone and contact new prospective clients and sponsors; or meticulously plan my week, for that matter.

Recently, I started creating structures around the things that I really want to accomplish but (for one reason or another) have not been following through. So, every week, I have someone who comes in so we can make calls and prospect. I have someone else who comes in so we can plan what I'm going to write as I make an attempt at my first book, yet someone else who helps me go over my week, think through my schedule and see where I can better spend my time based on what I say I want to accomplish most, and the project that is most interesting to me in the moment.

Having people around me who help hold me accountable allows me to more easily follow through on the things I consider important. Similarly, I think it's crucial for there to be a call to action at the end of any presentation created for the purpose of promotion and practice building. Since most doctors are not comfortable with the selling part of selling, bringing in someone who has that ability to wrap up the talk is crucial.

Simply lecturing like a professor in a college setting, where the bell rings and everyone rushes off to the next thing, is not an effective way to use speaking as a marketing tool. It's kind of like spending the day fishing and never baiting the hook because you don't like to touch worms. The talk should be fun, engaging, inspiring and educational, sure. But it must also get people to act. The more a speaker can connect their humanity and passion to the people sitting in their room, the better their response will be. But at the end, there has to be a call to action. You have to take people by the hand and walk them to the next step.

So please put the book down, find a yellow think pad, and take a few minutes to plan the offer that no one in your room will be able to refuse. If you get only one thing out of the time you invested reading this material, please make this it.

Why I Hate PowerPoint

When we first began producing events some ten years ago, most of our speakers did not have PowerPoint. They simply showed up and spoke. In a few years, there was one person who began bringing a projector, and before you know it, everyone else did as well. Certainly, it is a great tool and can be a terrific addition to highlight some visual points the speaker is making, but that screen can also become a wall behind which the speaker hides their fear and lack of preparation.

And how many times were there technological problems where the speaker spends the first 10 or 20 minutes of their talk frantically trying to get the PowerPoint to work, thinking that's the actual presentation, when nothing can be further from the truth. The presentation is not on the laptop but in you, the speaker's mind and soul.

We once had a renowned speaker come in to keynote our expo, for whom we set up a projector and screen for their PowerPoint. So there are some 500 people seated and standing in the back and around the walls excitedly waiting to hear their message. And the first thing he does, after I introduce him to enthusiastic applause and a warm reception, is play a ten-minute video. And although it was playing fine on the screen, we did not have a plug for the sound. So we ran the hand held mike to the speakers of the projector and tried to pipe the sound through the speakers above. After a few minutes of that, people started leaving the room. It was probably the most painful ten minutes of my life . . . except, maybe, when I bought my wife some kitchen utensils for her birthday. That was worse.

As soon as he started speaking, however, he quickly connected with the audience and spoke amazingly well for the next hour. If only he started with that, connected with the audience immediately, and began to ride the wave of excitement and enthusiasm that was palpable in the moment he walked on stage.

This technology is great to make a PowerPoint, but not to inspire or tell a story. That's your job.

Alex Lubarsky

I would Never Go See that Doctor

Once I brought in a consultant to evaluate the speakers who appeared at one of our larger events. This man had many years of experience working with speakers of all kinds and authored a book on the topic of leadership; he helped CEO's of Fortune 500 companies prepare for important presentations and improve their stage presence. Throughout the day, he attended about ten out of some fifty of our lectures. He had some interesting things to report that I thought would be helpful to all of us who are striving to share our message effectively.

One of the speakers had mostly text on her many slides. As she was going through her talk, she read a large portion of it directly from the screen and, at one point, had the audience read along. Another speaker wanted to turn everyone in his room into an honorary medical doctor, because he fired off so much information that he quickly lost his audience (if he ever connected with them in the first place), eventually running over his time into that of the following presenter. And yet another speaker spent most of the lecture sharing the story of his life, with little about what we can do to improve ours.

My evaluator said there was one doctor, who was speaking on a topic of great interest to him, but he felt so overwhelmed with technical information and scientific jargon, he confided in me that even though this doctor could probably help him, he would never go and seek their services.

On the other hand, he walked into a lecture where the topic was way out of his realm of interest and was only planning to stay for about ten minutes and scoot to another lecture happening simultaneously in the

88

next room. But this speaker was so engaging and brought her message to life with her animated presence while involving the audience at every opportunity, he found himself wanting to stay for the entire thing. Sure, she used PowerPoint, but only had about ten slides with a picture and a word or two of text to highlight her message and emphasize an idea. She did not use technology as a crutch that separated her from her audience, but used it in tandem to highlight important points she was making.

The purpose of the presentation is to give something of value to those who took the time to attend, connect with them on a personal level and remind them that no matter what the situation, there is always hope.

The Laws of Speaking

When I was about 14 years old, I took a car that my dad brought home from work and drove it to New Jersey with a bunch of my friends. It was a yellow cab that was ready to be signed off and put out to pasture after scurrying people around New York City for a few years, so all the things that made it a "TAXI" were removed. The roof lights, the meter on the dash, registration on the window and the medallion on the hood were all gone. This car was still yellow, but was not registered or insured and was of questionable mechanical integrity since it was no longer fit to be used as a cab. To add to this precarious situation, it was the middle of winter and the streets were covered with snow.

Once we got to New Jersey, I accidently made a left turn onto a one-way street running into a black and white police car headed the other way. He was far enough away that I was able to stop and realize what I had just done but not until we were standing virtually bumper to bumper. We looked at each other through our windshields, the officer and I, and

I could see the shock on his face as I am sure he saw on mine. I put the car in reverse and, nonchalantly, started to back up to the road from where I made the turn. It was not long before I heard the heart-stopping "whoop whoop" of his siren, telling me to pull over.

"Your license and registration," he said to me sternly. "I don't have either," I replied with a sheepish smile. After assessing the situation, I'm sure he knew that he had to put me and my buddies in jail and impound the car. There was just no other way around it. So till this day, I'm not sure why, but the next thing he said to me was: "Kid, I'm going to guide you out of this street. Go home, and don't ever do that again." Thank you, officer!

Speaking in public is kind of like driving a car, for it also has laws that we have to learn and abide by so we can do it well, be effective at it and keep ourselves out of trouble. Once I heard a new author do a presentation that was completely memorized. I've done that myself many times. It gives the impression of someone just reading, but instead of looking at a paper in front of them, they are looking at the text in their mind. Then there are some who just wing it; there is no preparation, the talk is not well thought out, so they are all over the place going from one topic to the next. I've done that plenty of times as well. People will usually begin a talk like that with something like: "I'm just going to speak from the heart."

The most effective way of preparing for a talk, I've found, is to memorize the outline, some of the important points and the quotes you want to stress. Then practice the presentation in front of a mirror (or a mentor) and do it enough times till you get the material deep in your mind and you know it and can recite it as easily as you can your ABC's. Zig Ziglar, the legendary motivational speaker and author, said that he can only do a good extemporaneous talk after practicing it a hundred or so times.

Once you get in front of an audience, you have to connect with them and humbly sell them on why listening to you will be of value to them. When you are connected with the people seated in front of you, there is an unmistakable (and very palpable) give-and-take of energy that a speaker will experience. It feels right once you are in that space, and if you are able to improvise as situations arise, be completely in the moment, and not lost in your own mind as you try to retrieve the text for the next thought, then that is the place where you can deliver your message with the most effect and seem like you are just talking to a few friends about a topic you know and one they find interesting.

To help better build positive energy in your room, you could ask someone you know to sit in the audience towards the front. They could be there as a welcome eye contact docking station, supporting and encouraging you as they smile and nod approvingly, which can help build your confidence and allow you to better connect to the rest of the people in the room.

Prior to going out on stage and facing your audience, it is also very helpful to create the right context in your mind and an empowered state in your body. Tony Robbins once shared an experience where he went into the bathroom to pound his chest and scream "YES" into a mirror to get into state, when a terrified man opened one of the stalls and quickly ran for the exit. When Billy and I first began speaking on the train, every time we started the day, the fear and doubt was so thick you could pull it out of the air and make cupcakes. That is, until the day when I wrote out a purpose statement and had each of us read it out loud to each other before speaking to the many commuters.

But, ultimately, all those laws can best be learned only if you get into the car and drive to New Jersey. To do something well, it's worth doing poorly at first. You have to get started and do it enough times so that you get past the fear, even if you feel that you're not ready or that you may, inadvertently, break some laws of rhetoric along the way.

Today, anytime our friends get together, they just point at me and say, "Alex, say a toast" since I have no fear of addressing any size group and can be completely in the moment. I can usually come up with something on the spot, pulling directly from the environment around me. And although I had to acquire my ability for extemporaneous speaking awkwardly, like a caveman trying to make fire, I have emphasized to my children and nieces the value of strong public speaking skills, so all of them today are exceptional in their confidence and ability to communicate in virtually any setting, and in front of any size group.

Learn From the "Greats"

Having attended at least a thousand seminars in my life, I've seen my share of speakers both good and awkward. It was there in those rooms with hundreds of people in attendance, I learned the styles of presentation that I wanted to emulate. Some were motivational and inspiring, others were deeply brilliant and technical, some were energetic and others emotional and profound.

Some presenters walked through the audience as they spoke, while others just stood behind the podium. There were very funny speakers, and there were serious speakers. And then there were some who I can still picture as they shared some revolutionary story that stayed with me and altered how I look at the world. But to me, the most effective speakers were those who shared their vulnerability and humanity as they connected to the audience. They used stories of personal events that moved them and made them who they are, and they were accessible, vulnerable, open and honest.

What was most interesting is that they all came from different backgrounds. Some were well-educated, while others dropped out of school. Some were from wealthy families, yet others were from humble beginnings. Some were shy and others outgoing. But the common denominator was that there was something important that they needed to share, and there was nothing that was going to stop them from sharing it. Not their own fear, not the nay-sayers, not circumstances and not personal tragedies. Usually, it was all of those things that they used to propel themselves forward and push past that awkward stage and into the zone.

What's the Next Stop

In all the years of doing marketing for the wellness community, the speakers would show up and speak and the exhibitors would show up and exhibit. Never has any one of them took the extra step of promoting their appearance, in addition to the marketing I provided, at the level of a young fellow I met a few years after we began doing our events. Howard Hoffman is the founder of pHresh Greens, a powdered supplement that's an organic compilation of 16 raw vegetables, sea algae and cereal grasses.

Starting this company on Long Island, New York with little but his own passion and work ethic, he took a booth at the NAVEL expo, and then went ballistic when it came to marketing. He brought renowned speakers as spokes-people for his product to the event and did lots of outside media and marketing to let people know that his representative was speaking at our event.

He was creative, proactive and did not wait for anyone to do it for him. Eventually, he took his company nationally, bringing his product to every major retailer from Walmart to Whole Foods across the nation. And although he later moved to California, his company exhibits continually at Health Media events. Today, he even has a mascot dressed in a full body suit that looks like a bottle of his very awesome and healthy greens. Go Howie!

Something to think about: *If you did not do today what terrified you yesterday; then tomorrow will be no different than the day before.*

Chapter 5

Do No Harm

"Do not spoil what you have by desiring what you have not; remember that what you now have was once among the things you only hoped for." — *Epicurus*

When I came home from school that day, the tiny one-bedroom where we lived was a mess. There were puddles of blood all over the worn, parquet floor of the living room. As I walked in hesitantly and looked around, each moment powered by raw emotion of concern mixed with fear, those minutes forever recorded on my mind like that of an 8mm film with some vintage video camera. Even now, some 35 years later, I can picture myself as a young boy of 11, putting my key in the faded and scuffed burgundy front door. I step inside. I see the blood; the daylight streaming in through our drape-less windows illuminating the bare, white-washed walls to the sides and the deep red blood below. I hear the sound of cars passing in the streets and a cacophony of voices floating up from the nearby playground. I can replay it at will; rewind it and see it again in slow motion, if necessary. Should I run? Call for help? Or cry? This was a bad day.

You may have experienced a day similar to the one I had so many years ago.

When someone we love is injured, whether by accident or incident, we have no idea how to react or what to do . . . except if we were medically trained. If we were a doctor.

We had just received the furniture that spent about six months crossing the Atlantic Ocean that my parents sent over from the former USSR just before embarking on the voyage to a new life ourselves. Till then, we were living pretty barebones, with whatever sparse furnishings— mismatched chairs, a tethered brown couch and a faded vinyl-top table—that charitable organizations were kind enough to donate. So my dad was pretty excited when finally our furniture arrived. He pried open the few crates and began to assemble the simple fixtures made with pride in the former soviet bloc. Many of the pieces did not fit, and the glass was slightly larger than the rim on the door of the cabinet that was meant to house it.

Sadly, mechanical inaptitude is genetic and is easily passed down from one generation to the next. That is why when something needs fixin' in my house, I call in the experts. But back then, there were no such frills available. My parents came to the United States in their early 30's with their two young children in tow and just a few hundred dollars to their name that our kind and all-knowing leaders of the Kremlin elite allowed them to take on this one-way journey. The rest (whatever they had accumulated over a lifetime till that point) had to be surrendered or used to purchase the ever-so-slightly uneven furniture stamped with the State Quality Mark of the USSR, and that (in all practicality) no one would otherwise willingly buy. Ever. And, of course, condoms; also made with pride and stamped with the same State Quality Mark. These rubber treasures were an important tradable commodity that the West needed and would pay handsomely for. We were told.

As my dad placed the door of the cabinet flat on that worn parquet floor, he tried to fit the glass into the rim that was off ever-so-slightly, pressing it with the palm of his hand and leaning just a bit much of his body weight into it. As the glass gave way, it exploded into a set of glass cutlery, slicing through the veins on the wrist of his left hand.

As both of my parents fled to the emergency room of a nearby hospital, somehow remembering to close the front door to our apartment behind them, they left the place looking like a crime scene. My dad is fine. He lives back in Moscow with my new mommy who is slightly older then my oldest child. But that is a story for another time.

This time I'd like to point out the incredible job doctors did in saving my father's life . . . and express my profound gratitude.

But what if those doctors were not there? Sure we expect them to be at our beck and call anytime we have a problem, but what if this was a world where they did not feel compelled to spend their days taking care of other people's problems? Or what if they were there, but they just were not any good at their job? The word 'inept' comes to mind. And also 'bureaucrat'.

I know it's hard to imagine because we've never known any different, but just for a minute, let you and I pretend that when our life is on the line there is no one there to save us.

The Richest Man in Washington State

As I type this, I am using the latest version of Microsoft Word, a program created by Bill Gates and the enterprise he founded. Bill lives in a 66,000 square foot estate, worth an estimated 147 million dollars. That is one big home, and much bigger than practically required to house him, his wife Melinda and their three children. Personally, I think that a 5,000 square foot home, worth 2 million would be perfectly fine. Don't you? In fact, perhaps we can argue that Bill makes way too much money and that the 11.5 billion he made in 2013 is a bit ostentatious. Perhaps, if we can pay him a million dollars, we could allocate the rest to many other important endeavors and projects that no one can argue are important, and he can still enjoy all the accolades and notoriety that comes from providing a product that many of us could not live without.

The only caveat in that thinking is, if that were the case, there would be no Bill Gates. Not as we know him at least. He would (in all probability) be some lonely bureaucrat in some secure government institution writing code that would never see the light of day. But personally, he could spend time traveling, relaxing, playing video games, wearing cool jerseys to popular sporting events and complaining about the state of the economy and how high the taxes are. In essence, we would not be killing the golden goose; we would have pretty much destroyed the environment in which the egg from where he hatched came.

The same goes for Angelina Jolie who, last year, took in 33 million dollars. For acting! Doing something she loves. Why can't we just pay her $500,000 —a substantial figure— and spend the rest on providing starving children around the world with food, for example.

I don't mean to make light of tragic situations that demand attention, but at the same time, I'd like to point out that both of the above examples are people who create something we value, giving the rest of us something to aspire to. If we know that (by capitalizing on our abilities, creativity and courage) we are unlimited in what we can achieve or have, many of us will sacrifice, grow, develop, practice and work harder than we would otherwise to pursue our dreams and not just settle for a safe, tenured job at the nearby post office. Because, ultimately, it is not about the millions we accumulate (or all the cool stuff this great country of ours can provide for us to enjoy), but it is the person we grow into in the pursuit of our dreams that matters most.

And finally, what about Jack Whittaker, who at 319.9 million dollars, was the biggest lottery winner in US history? Although, to me, lottery is simply a self-imposed sucker's tax, where usually the poorest among us put all of their hopes for a better life into just one of some 100 million tickets purchased by people with similar hopes. It's really bizarre that in this land of 'milk and honey', so many would put all their eggs for the realization of their dreams into that earth-sized, bottomless basket or all their balls for a future of life on their terms, into that giant air-mix lottery machine.

So what if we told Jack, who did not earn a penny of his new-found fortune, that out of his many millions he would get to keep one? It's still a lot of money. But would that motivate as many of these simpletons to line up and purchase a ticket next Week? I think not.

And what do the people above have in common other than their great fortune? None of them ever finished college. Neither did Mark Zuckerberg of Facebook (who is worth 33.3 billion) or Kobe Bryant (the NBA star who made 23 million dollars last year for playing basketball). And yet a doctor (who not only finished college, but went on for another ten years of study, sacrificing time and taking on huge loans so that they can provide a life-saving service that we all eventually need), has to live on relative minimum wage compared to a guy dribbling a ball down a court.

Incentive is what drives society forward; the pursuit of personal interests. The things I want is what gets me up in the morning. Sure, to paraphrase Zig Ziglar, I can have more of those things I want when I help and serve others so they can have the things they want. But, ultimately, if I did not want anything, I would not do anything. Maybe you're different.

Excuse Me . . . Are You a Doctor?

Since I have spent the last ten years of my life marketing integrative doctors, people have mistakenly addressed me as "Doctor Lubarsky", or (on numerous occasions) asked me if I am a physician. My usual answer is: "To the great disappointment of my mother, I am not a doctor of any kind". The reason I say that is because my mother had hoped that was what I would become . . . a famous physician. It was her dream for me. And for years, my dad would introduce me to everyone we met as his son "the future famous doctor". Last week, I asked him to please stop.

It was a nice gesture.

And I tried. In my spare time, I read the encyclopedia Britannica that my mom bought from a door-to-door sales person for a lot more money than she could afford at the time. So I looked up different topics on anatomy and medical terminology and tried to memorize the impossible-to-memorize words like: Pneumonoultramicroscopicsilicovolcanoconiosis, for example—an actual word meaning lung disease. I even applied to Stuyvesant High School— famous for its pre-med program— but did not make it in.

Looking back, it's easy to see why. Most of the kids in that room taking the entrance exam with me have been on that course from birth. They either had a supportive environment, a remarkable intelligence, an insatiable drive, or all three. They were completely prepared, trained and practiced; this was a course set for them (or one they set themselves) and this was just another planned stop on that journey. As for me, I was motivated sure, but had no background or understanding of the basics. The entire exam could have been in Greek, and I got most of it wrong, except for some obscure lung disease with a very long and impossible-to-pronounce word describing it. That I got right.

Doctor, It Hurts When I Do This . . .

At our events, we have some of the brightest physicians from around New York and the world who very generously give of their time and expertise, trying to educate those thousands of people who attend on the foundations of healthy living, prevention and wellness care. So there are lots of interactions. Some a little strange.

I was passing by the booth of one of our holistic dentists who was surrounded by a group of people peppering him with questions after his recent lecture, with one lady leading the charge. As I overheard it, she had a complaint about one of her teeth and wanted him to look at it and diagnose it right there, in the middle of this event. So she opened her mouth as if she were in a dental chair of some imaginary office with jazzy music softly permeating the air and no one else around but her and this startled doctor. She, like many of us from time to time, look to doctors in social situations to provide us the answer to a personal health problem plaguing us for years and causing discomfort.

Except today, this blatant lack of etiquette has gone viral, and the entire nation has organized itself in such a way that doctors are becoming less of the prized elite of our society, and instead (with a wave of a magical wand, some smoke and a few incantations by some politician, cackling and stirring the proverbial potion of doom in his black pot atop of a log fire), our doctors have become a new branch of the public sector similar to the misfits who work at your local DMV.

The Great Iconoclast

Some years ago, I was sitting in the office of one of my clients. He was a medical doctor who had practiced for some 40 years and his practice had evolved into a concierge model where he would integrate virtually any modality that would address the cause of the problem his many patients were dealing with. I remember sitting there lamenting about the state of health care and all the things I felt were wrong with it.

"There are way too many restrictions and regulations, the government is too deeply involved, there is no freedom for doctors and the entire model is controlled by insurance companies who are, in turn, controlled by the government; worse, the entire thing is focused on managing disease instead of helping people stay well, or get well by correcting underlying causes. In essence, doctors are not practicing medicine but maintaining the decaying infrastructure of the eternal Model T, one of the original Ford motor vehicles that you could have in any color, so long it was black. It's time to push that clunker to the nearest junk yard and unleash the brilliance and creativity of this elite group so they can help us become the healthiest, most-fit, and longest-lived people in the world."

He looked at me for a moment and said, "You know, Alex, you are an iconoclast." I usually make it a point to ask people for the meaning of a word they said if I don't know it. Ultimately, that is how I learned to speak English in the first place. He would not answer my question and just told me to look it up. So I did. An iconoclast is someone who opposes or criticizes beliefs and practices that are widely accepted. Sure, but I was like someone who was thrown into the ocean trying to tell the fish that there is an experience other than the one they have always known. A world that is different. One that they could not imagine, because a fish (no matter how smart or well-educated) has never been out of water. And if someone has lived in freedom and abundance all of their life, it's hard to imagine how it is to live without it. I tell my children (who grew up in the safe and beautiful suburbs of Long Island) that their entire life is a fairytale spent in some version of Disney World, and that it has little basis of reality or what life is like for most people on this planet.

A Portrait of Obama

Forward many years later. I was meeting with yet another doctor who has an office in Brooklyn, and who invited me to speak about possibly marketing his practice. The grand and palatial building he was in was built in 1927. The office had ten-foot ceilings and there were landscape oil paintings hung on the walls, all signed (I later noticed) by the doctor himself. There was also a portrait of President Obama on one of the bookshelves, along with something like a thousand volumes of medical text. The beautiful botanical gardens were literally across the street, and the area was bustling with people and activity. Definitely very impressive. And not that it matters, but this doctor also happened to be black.

He was very gracious and welcoming, and after the initial niceties, we sat down around an oak table in his meeting room and began to chat. First, I shared a bit about what I do and asked that he tell me a little bit about him, his practice and what he was hoping to achieve.

He was, definitely, speaking my language. Recently, he sent a letter resigning from all the insurance companies that he had worked with in the past. Because of all the restrictions, difficulty of reimbursement and bureaucracy, he had decided to take his practice in a different direction. Still accepting Medicare, and hoping to capitalize from their wellness initiative, he put a lot of stock into what this program was offering. The other, albeit much smaller side of his practice, was concierge. That is, he had similarly sent a letter to all of the patients he had acquired over some 30 years of practice, letting them know that although he was no longer accepting their insurance, they were welcome to continue using his services but now on a fee-for-service basis. His brochure outlined the costs, like that of a take-out menu in a local restaurant, and offered very clear and transparent options for those willing to entertain this new and bold approach.

As he continued to share his philosophy, I was getting really excited about the possibility of helping position this practice in front of the kind of people who would most appreciate the exclusive attention and time from an experienced (and obviously, very caring) doctor. I was already getting a little ahead of myself, thinking what I would suggest about possibly polishing his image, and the media I would explore to put his free-market practice in gear.

Then he said something to me that pulled the proverbial needle across the vinyl record playing romantic music, bringing it to a screeching halt. "The answer to the health care situation in America," he said softly, "is a One-Payer System." Wait. You mean like the government collecting a gadjillion dollars in taxes and paying the doctors for services rendered directly? That kind of One-Payer System? You mean, where we place politicians (those kind, munificent and selfless servants of the public) in control of even more of our money and a crucial part of our economy, and life? The same mercurial government that is constantly riddled with scandal and ineptitude, debt and waste, lies and misinformation, secrecy and deceit; *that* government? You would rather take the control of the health care system from the greedy corporate bureaucrat and hand it over to the bumbling drones in the public sector? *Are you out of your mind*? I thought to myself, hoping my face did not betray what I was thinking.

"Doctor," I said finally, after regaining composure and stuffing my Russian temper back into the brick-walled cage with claw marks all over its aging walls and teeth indentations on the thick, metal bars of the heavily-fortified door.

"Are you sure that is the best option?" I asked with a smile.

"I was born in soviet Russia and we had 'free', government-run health care there. In fact, everything was free. Kind of like it is in prison. It is not a good system. It is equality at the level of poverty and I would rather have you, on your worst day, in charge of health care than our most wonderful politician on her best."

Who would have known that he was leading the charge of an organization heavily involved in pushing this One-Payer idea forward?

And with that (after a few more minutes of polite chatting), the doctor got up, shook my hand and thanked me for dropping by. If only I could hold my tongue and talk like the politicians, I would have most likely had a new account. But I can't do it. If the underlying philosophy is off, there is no way I can help someone attached to the security blanket of working for the government become a successful entrepreneur. It's kind of like proposing marriage to a nun sworn to celibacy. What can I possibly say to entice her to join me under the Chuppah?

One of the many things that makes this country great is that we have the opportunity to earn and pay for everything we may need or want. Sure, in some instances, people need help. My family were those people for a time, and as a society, we are always willing to support those who need to transition and become earners so they can pay their way, grow, evolve, develop and enjoy the fruits of their labor and the pride that comes with being of service. The problem, many times, is priority.

What do we consider more important in our society? The services of highly-trained professionals, or the shiny trinkets that everyone seems to have and wants more of?—The latest cell phones, expensive cars, flat screen TV's and cable. You would be hard-pressed to find someone in our metropolis who does not have those basics items for survival, but when you tell them that they need to pay to go see a doctor, they balk and say that it should be I who should pay for them; well, when I go to see my doctor, I think that they should pay for me. So there. That is the direction our society is going. We want to have it all, but have it paid by someone else. Or, as Frederic Bastiat, a French political economist said so much more succinctly:

"The state is that great fiction by which everyone tries to live at the expense of everyone else."

And that, my friend, is a recipe for a 'strawberry Jell-O with an arsenic base at a family reunion' kind of disaster.

Health Care Is Un-affordably Free

As a nation, we recently decided to place our health care system in the hands of the government, primarily because many people are not able to afford the price of coverage. Over 40 million don't have health insurance, we were told. The insurance plans are becoming way too expensive, they empathized. The heartless insurance companies don't accept those with pre-existing conditions (or charge them higher premiums if they do). Employers are shifting more of the expense on the employee, and the deductibles are growing astronomically.

But this particular answer to this particular problem was originally caused by the answer itself. It was a skewed government law around the Second World War that, over the last seventy years, grew and compounded into the problem that we are looking to solve with what caused it in the first place. It's kind of like, inadvertently, planting an oak seed in the ground and (years later, when it grows a hundred feet tall and blocks the sun) attempting to fix the no sun problem by planting more oak seeds.

It was a difficult time, to say the least, when the government implemented wage controls on all US corporations to curtail the siphoning of scarce talent from other companies. The world was at war and desperate times called for doing what-was-necessary-to-survive kind of measures. It would be arrogant to try and question what those times warranted or what was done, even with hindsight as a guide, and one with perfect vision.

Corporations got creative, as business people and entrepreneurs tend to be, and began looking for other ways to attract a talented work force by creating incentives that were not wage-related. So health insurance made all the sense in the world. It was relatively inexpensive, could be paid for with pre-tax dollars, yet the value it provided (whether true or perceived) made it a strong tool to leverage the interest of the most talented potential employees. It was the perfect arrangement and (when doctors mostly put band aids on cuts and prescribed two aspirin and a morning call as the main protocol in their approach to healing) the system worked excellent.

Today, of course, the landscape is very different. From MRI's to heart transplants, brain surgery and nanotechnology, DNA testing and artificial growth of limbs, medicine has grown too large and complex for the restraints that were placed on it when it was in its infancy and before we entered the space-age of medical care.

Health Care in Elephant's Clothing

Over a century ago, on a warm spring day, thousands of jubilant people of all ages headed to a small town nearby, where (on a large open field and under a big top) one of the biggest circus groups of its time were ready to thrill the eager crowds.

Not long into the program, as all attention was on the woman walking the high-wire near to top of the tent, a fire broke out near the animal cages, quickly spreading to the top covered with a highly flammable water-proofing material. As panic ensued, and everyone ran for their life, some of the animals who could not escape or be saved, sadly lost their lives. Many were in cages and could not escape. But the mystery lies with a large African elephant whose back leg was tied by a thin chain to a small stake in the ground; one that he could have easily pulled out and ran to safety. Surprisingly, however, he perished as well.

To solve this riddle, we have to go back to a time when this elephant was just a pup. There he was tied by the same thin chain, to the same small spike, similarly hammered into the ground. Try as he may to break free, he was not able to do it. He did not have the strength, although he had plenty of desire. And after some time, he stopped trying concluding that it was not possible. And what becomes impossible in our mind similarly becomes impossible in our world.

Today, like that elephant, our health care is tied by a thin chain to a small spike hammered into the ground, with the fires of change raging all around. But it, like he, cannot move because you don't believe you can. And unless you awake that passion that was deep within, having you do all the things people said were impossible, their challenge only spurring you on to rip through the chains holding you back. If you don't stir from this state of hypnosis, then our system of care is destined to a similarly gruesome fate.

Prior to the implementation of the Un-Affordable Care Act that many are hoping is the final step to that One-Payer System (where doctors are paid directly by the Federal government), some 94% of the health care expense was already paid for by a third party, (like the government or the strictly regulated insurance companies), shackled with over 1800 mandates, making private insurance nothing more than an extension of another stealthy entitlement program. And this fact created numerous problems. The first is what Paul Zane Pilzer, in his groundbreaking book, *The Wellness Revolution: How To Make a Fortune in the Next Trillion Dollar Industry,* calls *elastic demand*. When something is offered for free, or is perceived to be free, demand goes up. Perhaps kind of like placing a mountain of hundred dollar bills in the middle of Times Square. How many times will you need to replenish it until the crowd is satiated and stops taking it? Probably forever. The more money you pile on, the more demand you inevitably create.

The way to curtail demand is to raise the cost. So when anyone can go see a physician and they don't have to pay anything (or practically anything) and have no concept of what it costs or should cost, the insatiable appetite of demand will only grow. So our health care system becomes the finite, all-you-can-eat buffet for the infinite demand of a frenzied public with a ravenous and unquenchable appetite.

The second problem is that the entire system is mired in obscurity and mystery. When we go to the doctor, are the costs clear like when we go to the supermarket? Why not? Are things made simple for us to understand or is everything purposely complex, so that we won't bother?

And how do our brilliant leaders untangle this hair ball? They take over the entire health care system, some 16% of our economy and the most valuable part or a person's life, and bureaucratize further.

The Coming Two-Tier Health Care System

According to a New York Times article by Dr. Scott W. Atlas, who is a medical doctor, professor at Stanford University Medical Center and author of numerous books on the topic including *"Reforming America's Health Care System: The Flowed Vision of ObamaCare",* the greatest irony of a draconian government system to control health care will create some unintended consequences. Now that everyone is forced into the same health system of care, those of us in the middle class or lower will mostly have no choice in the matter. But people who usually fly first-class or have access to Air Force One, for example, will most likely choose a more individualized approach to health care for themselves and their families. So a compulsory system designed to provide a version of affordable housing for all will inevitably force a segment of our society to purchase luxury dwellings that provide highly attentive, bespoke, cutting-edge health care.

You can see it now. There are hundreds of doctors that I know personally who do not accept insurance of any kind and to see them, people have to pay out of pocket, and usually a substantial amount. But interestingly, you would think that it is the wealthy who seek out this kind of care exclusively. In many instances, that image is warped by those who put a higher value on their health than trying to keep up with the luxurious lifestyle of the infamous Jones'. This growing segment of the population has become frustrated because the only kind of care available to them and their children is the "Let's wait until you are sick, and then we'll see you for 3.27 minutes, prescribe some symptom-suppressing chemical concoction, and for the duration of your life, valiantly manage the original disease and the side-effects of the treatment." But at least it's free. That is an ineffective system that not only focuses all of its resources on the management of existing conditions, but it creates the perfect ecosystem, however unintentional, to assure its virus-like dissemination.

Of course as a business model, this kind of care is very successful, to the tune of some three trillion dollars per year. It would make Mr. Evil smile with pride had he thought of this diabolical plot. All one has to do is provide ongoing treatment and manage (but not cure) the growing wave of chronic diseases that afflict an ever-expanding contingent of the population and then get someone (who is everyone and, therefore, no one) to pay the million-trillion dollars for it . . . "Yea, baby, that's groovy!"

"And, it's *'Doctor Evil'*. I did not spend six years in Evil Medical School to be called 'Mister', thank you very much."

Except today, that gentle wave of disease has grown into what looks more like a tsunami, affecting virtually everyone in our society. It has become difficult to contain and threatens the destruction of the very system that fostered it, primarily because of its success. Perhaps like in the movie *The Patriot*, where the ruthless British Colonel Tavington of the Green Dragons set out to kill the family and friends of Benjamin Martin, an American patriot played by Mel Gibson; as the Colonel's over-the-top cruelty unintentionally unleashed a fury that, ultimately, resulted in his own demise.

Similarly, that fighting spirit has been unleashed in people like Suzanne Somers, Carol Alt, Mark Hyman and Fran Dresher, all of whom experienced the trauma of a life-threatening disease and became outspoken champions for the creation of a new and better approach to care. Of course, more and more medical doctors are also finding their way through the labyrinth of propaganda illuminated by the lucid vision of a personal health crisis. This awakening is happening throughout our society as more of us realize that, unless we do something to reverse this frightening trend, it will be the self-inflicted health problems (and not some foreign enemy or even the looming economic collapse) that will be the cause of our downfall.

The Two Shysters with an Invisible Cloak

Every summer, and for many years, my wife and I would send our children to an intimate, upstate New York camp for Russian children near the Canadian border. The woman who founded it, studied and taught theater in Moscow, so each year they would pick a topic (a book or a play) and create their version of it. The kids sewed costumes and built a backdrop on the porch of the picturesque, five-bedroom house that is camp. And towards the end of the summer, along with the parents and family of the other 25 or so children, we set out on a long, five hour trip to see the kids and this way off Broadway production.

This particular year, my son was playing one of the two shyster tailors who were trying to sell a king on a robe that would be unlike anyone has ever seen. In fact, this particular outfit can only be seen by the smartest, the wisest and the most elite.

So there he was on that porch-stage, in his what-a-tailor-would-look-like-at-the-time outfit, sewing his invisible thread through an invisible cloak for the exuberant king, played by one of the chubbier kids. Once dressed, his royal highness examined himself in the mirror approvingly, as those around him tried to outdo each other in proving just how smart, wise and elite they were because they were the ones able to see and appreciate this invisible outfit. So everyone was in agreement and everyone was seeing what really wasn't there, because they were afraid to see anything else.

As the king came out to greet the public who lined the streets of a mock parade, everyone was saying to anyone within earshot how beautiful the king's outfit was. Everyone, that is, except the one young boy who held his mother's hand and looked confused. All of a sudden, he looked up, pointed, and exclaimed, "Mommy, the emperor has no clothes!"

So it is for me. There are very smart, well-educated and clearly intelligent people who have been sold on an idea that is this backward system; one focused on the endless management of disease, unable to address the underlying problem, and that's quickly becoming economically unsustainable—the way for us to go if simply it was run by the government.

Whereas, I'm just standing on the side (like that young boy), my eyes wide with amazement as I point out that the emperor has no clothes, and that this health care system makes no sense.

Something to think about: *Those who don't understand marketing will always be at the mercy of those who do.*

Chapter 6

The Magic of Thinking Bigger

"If things seem under control, you are just not going fast enough." — ***Mario Andretti***

If you have never been to Rhode Island, I'd like to encourage you to go. The picturesque drive down Long Island (at times on a thin, two-way road with endless ocean views on either side), a quick ride on the Martha's Vineyard Ferry from Orient Point of the North Fork to New England, Connecticut, and before you know it, you've entered a quaint world with suspension bridges, water views, sail boats, mansion-museums built by the titans of industry past, lovely towns, shops and "mom & pop" restaurants.

The first time we went there, we were invited by a couple who we've been friends with for many years. They had rented a home near the beach and we joined them for the weekend, together with our five-year-old son.

He, like me, is a lifelong entrepreneur, and she (his high school love with a great sense of humor) was studying interior design. We had a fun time exploring the area and lunching in some of the restaurants with outside seating. One day, we spent on the beach, which was a short walk from where we stayed. After unfolding our chairs and pushing the wooden spike of the umbrella into the sand, we sat down to relax.

At the same time, my son ran closer to the water with his blue plastic shovel that had a two-foot long wooden handle and began to build a sand castle, his favorite activity at the beach. My friend and I sat there chatting as the girls did the same nearby. After a while, my buddy (who has a philosophy that says, "Since when do you have to be hungry to eat?") suddenly got up from his chair (not something he would do unless absolutely necessary) and walked over to where my son was busy at work building his version of the Leaning Tower of Pisa.

My friend asked the boy to let him borrow his shovel and began to dig a circumference around the castle that resembled a smaller version of a crop circle. As he continued to dig the outline, some of the other children nearby stopped what they were doing and began to watch with curiosity what this big kid was up to. As the foundation to this almost life-size castle began to take shape, the children started to walk toward it as if pulled by some invisible magnet. They had their toy shovels in hand and asked if they could help. Once my friend has his team in place, all very excitedly working together on this bigger-than-life project, he nonchalantly walked back to his beach chair and sat back down.

This year, my friend's business is poised to do a hundred million dollars in revenue.

His innate ability to see things on a bigger scale inspires the people around him to want to be a part of anything he endeavors. And sure, he's smart, but so are you. The only thing he has going for him above most struggling entrepreneurs, is that he envisions everything so big that it would frighten the average person. And the other very important thing he has is the uncanny belief that he will succeed in whatever he gets involved with, so usually he does.

The Power of Belief

There are many books written on the topic of belief. One of the best is *The Magic of Thinking Big* by David J. Shwartz, PhD, who says, "Believe You Can Succeed and You Will." But that is like saying get behind the controls of a 747 jetliner and you will fly. Sure, you can do it. You have the tools to do it, but what you need to do to get that thing off the ground will take a deeper knowledge of how belief works.

Personally, I stumbled onto a false belief many times in my life. Sometimes I had to get rid of one belief, something I was sure was true but experience proved otherwise, and then had to create a new belief in its place, one that better supported the direction I wanted my life to go. At times, I was able to recognize my view as faulty myself. Most times, however, it was pointed out to me by the either a book, a seminar or the people closest to me.

Napoleon Hill in his classic book *Think and Grow Rich* said, "Whatever the mind of man can conceive, it can achieve"; but I'm sure he meant that only if that man believes that he can achieve that what his mind conceived. So where does belief comes from and how do we bring its magic power to serve and help bring our dreams to life?

119

Certainly, as parents, we can help build a strong system of belief and self-confidence in our children. We can mold their minds and thought process to know that they can succeed in whatever endeavor they choose to get involved with, and we can also teach them the basics of that process. But only if we are confident enough ourselves to give that gift of belief to them and teach them how to create new, empowering ones at will. What then, if our parents were not able to give us those foundations because they did not have them to give? How do we build that precious and tenuous power within our own soul (so like the sharp edge of an axe) we are able to cut through virtually any obstacle set in our path?

When I was in my early teens, I was already working in my dad's taxi shop on a semi full time basis. And before I share this story, let me just say that I was not an easy child. After going through the immigration process and the emotional toll that it took, I had become an angry, unhappy, unsmiling and no self-image-to-speak-of kid. I was never a bad guy, but if trouble was around the corner, I would usually go out of my way to make the turn. So I am sure that, at that time, I did not exactly inspire confidence as someone who would amount to much.

I remember walking up the staircase that lead to the office of the shop where we worked. My dad happened to be walking down, so he stopped me to give some instructions about something. After he finished, I shared with him that in a few years I want to open my own auto body shop and specialize in repairing exotic cars that were in an accident. I can clearly remember the expression on his face as he looked at me and said, "You are too stupid to start your own business."

It's those kind of emotionally-charged thoughts carved into the grey matter of a child's mind that drive their actions for many years to come; like demon voices constantly whispering in the ear, eating away at the belief system and undermining the ability to create the life envisioned. So if you were able to have a confident family that provided you with uplifting and encouraging ideas as they create the kind of nurturing environment for you to thrive, I think that is an amazing advantage and one not enjoyed by most of the world's population. On the other hand, if you're like most people who are not so fortunate, then you can use the strength, tenacity and experience you gained from digging yourself out of that dump to build something magnificent with your life.

Interestingly, each new endeavor requires its own set of beliefs. So if one happens to be a confident doctor, lawyer, computer programmer, chef or auto mechanic, it takes a whole new set of beliefs should they endeavor to start a business and become an entrepreneur.

Time Keeps on Ticking

The most important ingredient in creating a new empowering belief is time. Once you change course and begin heading in a new direction, you have to give yourself the time necessary for the new belief to take root and grow. It's kind of like learning a new language. You can't expect to read a dictionary, buy a beret with a matching scarf, and go to Paris speaking fluent French. It is a process that demands time and patience. Even reciting your ABC's would be challenging if I asked you to do it backwards. Let's give it a shot: Z,Y,X,W . . . V . . .U . . .

Developing the belief that you can speak in public takes time. Developing the belief that you can sell from the stage takes time. Believing that you have everything you need to start and succeed in your own business takes time. If you pull the plug before the new belief you are trying to create has the time necessary to set, perhaps like a newly-paved sidewalk or a foundation to a building, it simply won't have the integrity to support your dreams as you move forward.

Recently, I met with a successful attorney who stopped being an attorney, quit his job and started an organic food delivery business. I also met a lovely, young lady who left a high-paying corporate job to teach a fitness class and created her own brand with a growing following. A close friend of mine gave up his medical degree to become a very successful international businessman. All of these people believed they could be successful in the pursuit of their life's passion before they could gather enough courage to move toward this new goal.

So if you don't like what you are doing now, if you go to work simply to pay bills, and if there is something you know you can create that will be a honest extension of your true self, then I believe it is also something you can be very successful in doing and it's something you must work towards if you are to truly be happy and satisfied. We spend a very large portion of our life working. It boggles my mind that any intelligent person would spend their entire life doing what they hate, simply to afford the things they don't really need so that they can impress people they don't really like.

Don't Mess With My Grey Matter

It is said that if you were to try and create a computer to equal the power of your mind, it would take up enough space to fill the empire state building and would need the Niagara Falls to cool it. Although perhaps with today's technology it would take less space and can be cooled with a less intimidating body of water, the point is that our mind is very powerful and is capable of remarkable creativity and accomplishment. But like a computer, there is the hardware, the raw materials we were given (be they ever so humble) and the software— those programs we, ourselves, choose to install and open for a particular task. Similarly, I can go back throughout my life and think about all the times I was told that I did not have what it takes to succeed. I remember speaking with my science teacher, a short lady with large hips and a long, black pony tail. I told her that I wanted to become a doctor to which she smiled empathetically and said, "The only thing you can hope for is to become average." And I'm not sure why, but that thought came up for me, in its many variations, throughout my life.

So the thoughts that were inadvertently placed in our minds by people of authority are the software that drives our lives forward. They are the strands of which our subconscious mind crafts the cables of belief. Eventually, over time, those cables become very difficult to break because you no longer see them as false beliefs, but the reality of your life. There is the sunset, the sunrise, and the fact that you can never succeed as an entrepreneur. You can't sell or sing. And you never finish what your start. Each is just as real, and just as impossible to see, as anything but fact.

The good news in all this is that, no matter how powerful the thoughts placed in our mind are, we have the ability to change them. We can begin to unravel those cables, one strand at a time, and begin to braid new ones out of thoughts that empower the life we choose to live and the endeavors we choose to pursue.

Thoughts Are Things, But Words Are the Tools That Mold Things

Once we become adults, we can no longer blame our environment for our failures because we have the power to change that environment. Of course, we can use that power to simply affirm the disempowering thoughts in our mind, or we can use it to craft our own more empowering ideas. What we say—the words we choose to speak, the ideas we verbalize each time we talk to a friend, to a group or to ourselves— is another opportunity to lay a strand towards the belief we wish to embody. "I can start my own business. I can learn anything that I need to learn to be successful. If another person has done what I wish to do, then I can do it as well. I am a powerful force in the world, and I have everything I need to create everything I want. My mind is a super computer with endless possibilities."

When we hear negativity, it affects us. When we hear it in the morning, it creates the context for our day. When we hear it as a child, it creates the context for our life. So we must become diligent, as soon as we are able, to remove all negativity from reaching our mind. Stop watching television, cancel the newspaper, if there are people in your life who put you down, make you doubt yourself or your dreams, get away from them. Life is way too short to spend it in the negative garbage dump of our own making.

Growing up in Soviet Russia, there were only three state-controlled channels on TV, all with the same guy telling us that our nation, once again, exceeded the five-year plan for growing wheat or potatoes or some other nonsense delivered in a somber tone by a stoic face. So naturally, as a kid, I had no interest in watching it. Only on Saturday at 6 pm

124

did they show cartoons for 15 minutes. So my friends and I dropped what we were doing and ran home to watch the animated version of indoctrination. Other than that, we played outside with whatever we could use as a toy. A very popular game in the neighborhood was called 'banka' where you find a stick and some cans; then you throw the stick at the cans and the more you knock down, the higher rank you got. Once you make General, you win. Of course, there was one kid who had a soccer ball, and when he came out we played soccer.

When we came to America, I discovered real television— from *Tom and Jerry* to *Bugs Bunny, The Flintstones, The Jetsons, Gilligan's Island, I Love Lucy, I Dream of Jeannie, Knight Rider*, etc. I was in heaven. And I spent hours watching it. I came home from school and would watch TV from 3pm to 9pm, then (if I had any strength left) I would do my homework. On Saturday, *Mighty Mouse* was on at 6 am followed by Saturday morning cartoons, 3 pm *Kong Fu* movie, and the rest of the weekend was pretty much the same. I was a TV addict. But that is just my personality. When I start doing something, I get addicted to it and the only way for me to break the addiction is to stop cold turkey. So the first thing I did when we had our first child, was cancel all cable service and disconnect the TV. I no longer purchased newspapers and became very careful of what I allowed to enter my mind and influence my thoughts.

All of those things have the ability to depress us because the media takes all the horrible things that people do (or search the world for the ugliest side of humanity) and then burn it into your mind with a digital version of a sand blaster, affecting your thoughts, your attitude and the paradigm from which you see the world.

Really, that is the only thing we can control. Our thoughts, our attitude and, to some extent, our actions and, as an entrepreneur, your mind, positively charged, is your greatest asset. So feed it inspiring ideas. Read the books of those whose life inspires you. When you drive, use that time to listen to audio books or some motivational and uplifting CD's. Take away the power of the world to control what you're thinking. Don't be a mental anorexic or a morbidly obese negativity junky when it comes to how you feed your mind and soul. Be as healthy, fit and nimble in your creative mind as you are in the body that carries it around.

Ultimately, the world communicates with you through your outer ear and can definitely influence your behavior. Just look at how people eat. Everything they see on television, they ultimately purchase when they go to the market. When people say they prefer brand names over generic, they are just saying that they want to buy what has been sold to them through the media; completely buying the message that was presented, regardless of how much sense it makes to support their goals for a healthy life or a fit body. Your inner ear, however, is your direct access to your own mind, kind of like a USB inserted directly into the hard drive. It's your best chance to install the kind of thinking that can drive you in the direction you once envisioned for yourself as an innocent child; one full of dreams and a limitless imagination. It is the words you say out loud, either to a friend or a mirror, that is probably ten times more powerful than anything anyone said to you in the past or tries to say to you now.

What You See Is What You Get

Do you remember how, as a child, you had these grand dreams for your life? I would guess that your reality today is very different than the one you once imagined. But you have to admit that it was fun to let our minds visualize being the President, an astronaut, a fireman, a famous doctor, a wealthy business person with our own island in the Caribbean, or all of the above. Since my daughter was able to talk, she wanted to be a teacher, an artist, a dancer and a mommy of twelve. Yea, good luck with that.

Then, as we got older, we began to learn things like gravity, Newton's law of motion, stop signs, passports, speed limit, rules, regulations, and realities of the world. Over time, we slowly stop using our imagination because it has disappointed us repeatedly, and we lean heavier on our practical, analytical mind. Instead of using our greatest power to imagine a world as it could be, we begin to think ourselves into the confines of the reality we find ourselves in, and a world as it is. In essence, we give up our power to create and trade it in for the ability to store and analyze information. We went from being an extension of God and His creative power to some version of an encyclopedia, a file cabinet or a junk drawer.

But just because we were not successful in matching our life with those things we imagined as a child, does not mean we should just shelf our most powerful tool, our imagination. The ability to envision a future we wish to live in, to see ourselves as someone different than who we are today, is what ultimately pulls us in that direction. And when we use the words we, ourselves, say to guide that imagination, as we feel the emotions of the imagined experience— one we create solely in our mind— that combination is the Love Potion # 9 as it regards your ability to create the beliefs and, eventually, the reality that becomes yours.

Leap Before You Look

Standing barefoot on a 50-foot cliff, there was ocean as far as I could see. The waves were slamming against the wall below as I tried to steady my nerves.

A group of us were spending a week in Negril, Jamaica, a tropical paradise surrounded with a clear, blue ocean, soft beaches, waterfalls, and cliffs from where the locals dove from heights that made one's heart beat faster just watching.

This day, we went to the world famous Rick's Café. It was on a cliff overlooking the horizon, an endless ocean, a spectacular sunset, and a place where the guests could jump into the ocean if they wanted to. As soon as we got there, my friends asked me if I was going to do it.

No!

I am not planning to jump, I said to myself. I'm dressed to go out for the evening and not for life-defying stunts. But before I knew it though, I took off my shirt and my shoes, pulled up my pants and got on the platform from which others were jumping. Usually, overthinking this kind of situation will prevent one from taking action. This has always been my experience, so usually I take the action, and worry about the details on the way down. I'm not talking about being reckless. There were other people who had done it before me, so it was relatively safe. Just taking action before the reasonable mind has a chance to justify the fear is a way to make sure you do the things that frighten you, and those things you know you should. Even though, the first time I took a step forward to jump, I stopped myself to take a peek down. It was a very long drop. On my second attempt, I was falling feet first, flailing my arms as if doing it fast enough was going to somehow slow me down. When I finally reached the water, I was still in the humming bird position and, as I hit the inside of my arms against the wavy top of the ocean,(one that felt more like wet cement), it almost, instantaneously, turned my skin black and blue.

There were a couple of hundred people watching as they sipped on their umbrella covered, alcoholic drinks, and when I came back up the stairs that were cut into the cliff, there were some faint applause.

I saw my friends smiling faces as they raised their drinks in my direction. And to my surprise, on that same cliff, I saw a young girl (maybe 14-years-old) ready to jump. I turned to a couple next to me and exclaimed, "Wow, that girl is going to jump!" "I don't think so," the guy answered. "She has been here for hours. She gets up on the cliff, stands there for a minute, looks down and then gets off. She will never jump," he finally asserted.

And, as if on cue, she got off the platform.

With that, I went up to the dad, who was there trying to encourage his daughter. I asked him if he would mind if I talked to her. "Sure," he said. "But I promise you that everyone has tried. She is just paralyzed by fear."

"Hi, what's your name?" I asked.

"I'm Jess," she answered.

"Mind if we chat?"

"Yea, sure."

"Why do you want to jump?"

"Well, all of my family jumped, and it's kind of expected that I do it, I guess."

"Sure, I get that. But why do YOU want to jump?"

She thought about it for a minute, looking over towards the edge where someone else was about to make the plunge. "Well, I guess I know if I jump and break through the fear, I will be able to do it in other areas of my life."

"Yes, that is exactly it, Jess. Most people live their entire lives never crossing that imaginary chasm from desire to action because of fear. People don't really live their lives fully because they are afraid to. And here, you have the opportunity to set the course for your entire life. So don't do it for your family or any of the people here. In reality, the very fact that you got on that edge and were willing to jump off a 50-foot cliff showed a tremendous amount of courage; and no one will think less of you if you choose not to do it."

I could see the expression on her face change from despondency to one of determination. So I said good bye and went back to the table where my friends were sitting to watch what happens. Within a few minutes, Jess was back on top of the platform. She took a step forward and stopped, retreating to the original start position. One of the fellows behind her offered his hand to help her back down off the edge. I could feel the struggle in her mind, but if she was ever going to overcome her fear and break through whatever it was holding her back, it would have to be her decision. Once again, she steadied herself, took a few steps forward and leaped off the side.

The entire atmosphere at the café changed instantaneously. It was charged with excitement as people pointed and looked at each other in mild disbelief. When Jess finally came up the stairs, soaking wet and with a big smile that she tried to restrain, the entire place erupted in cheers and applause.

So courageous and consistent action is an important ingredient in building a solid belief system, and you can either wait until you believe to take the action, or you can take the action so that you can believe.

Back at the airport, we were standing on a long, snaking line to board the plane that would take us back to New York when I heard someone closer to the front say excitedly, "That's the guy!" When I looked up, I saw my new friend, Jess, pointing her finger in my direction. "That's the guy who got me to jump!"

Thanks buddy, but it was all you.

The Dog Did Not Bark

On numerous instances, I have been accused of being credulous, a bit too trusting of people, and looking at the positive side of every person and situation I encounter. My wife calls me a Pollyanna, that girl character in the famous book by the same name, who always tried to find something to be glad about in everything.

I think that people, in most cases, try to be good. We lean towards doing the right thing although, at times, we can be pulled in a more sinister direction. I believe it is like that and not the other way around. So when I come into a new encounter, I think that the person is honest, smart, and has my best interest at heart. From there, it's not so much what they say, but what they do, that I focus on. Did they show up when they said they would? Did they do what they promised? Did they share pertinent information that may not be in their best interest and that I may have never found out about? Did they follow through on a commitment even though circumstances made it much easier not to?

All of these things become evidence that I gather to, hopefully, prove my case. After some time, as the pile of evidence grows, so does my belief about the kind of person they are and, eventually and hopefully, I convict them as being awesome.

But interestingly, the way we are with some people and situations, is not how we are in others. So certainly the way people see us and treat us becomes the context for our behavior. Another way of saying it is that some people and situations are able to bring out our best and others our worst. The question then, is how do we behave when we are just with ourselves? How do you see yourself and how do you behave when there is no one else around to influence that behavior? What kind of a person do we bring out in ourselves? You most definitely spend more time with yourself than anyone you know. And even if you are a terrific actor and you can fool me and those in your circle, you will have a much more difficult time pulling the wool over your own eyes for an extended period because, ultimately, you are always there as you conspire to do it.

This is where that opportunity to build belief comes in full force; as we begin to gather evidence to convict ourselves that we are headed in the direction that we say we want to go.

So how we think, what we say, and the actions we take on a daily basis helps to create the kind of beliefs that helps us be more effective and confident in the situations we find ourselves in. Those empowering paradigms from which we see and experience the world, and more importantly, the people in our world, is what ultimately helps drive us in the direction of a destiny we ourselves map. This is my belief, and one that inspires the actions that I took today and will take tomorrow.

Over the years, I have always tried to provide more service than I promise. So even if the person I'm speaking with does not know it, my intention is that, after we agree on the terms, I will do much more for them than I said I would or was contracted to do, especially in the early stages of our relationship. So I don't really need an office with fancy furniture or walls full of diplomas to create the context and credibility I need. I am confident because I have done this enough times. My belief is: whoever I happen to be working for or the endeavor I happen to find myself in, I will work myself very hard and make investments no one expects me to make, just to assure I did everything possible to deliver on my promise and then some.

I have also learned that most people don't think that way. So when I meet someone with this attitude, I treasure them and that relationship. Surrounding myself with like-minded people helps reinforce my beliefs and allows me the most authentic way to live and experience life.

Repetition Is a Mother

According to Malcom Gladwell's book, *The Outliers*, once you learn the basics of a particular skill, everything takes a back seat to practice, including talent and natural ability. Looking at the career of people like the Beatles, he explains that mastery comes at about 10,000 hours of practice time. Certainly, one can take their entire life to get that many hours of practice under their belt, or as in the case of John Lennon and his crew, it was some 1200 concerts over a period of just 4 years, seven days a week at as many as 8 hours per day. Their superior sound wasn't just born; it was crafted over time and consistent practice.

This is great news for all of us who are embarking on a new journey in our life. Once we find something that we are passionate about, something we naturally want to do and don't really consider work, then all we have to do is create the environment where we can get ourselves to practice that skill as often as possible until we become clearly proficient at it. So as you practice continually, at the same time, you also build your belief that you are someone who is willing to do what is necessary so as to master your craft. As this belief solidifies, you practice more and the former continues to feed the latter.

Once you really decided to move forward towards your dream of becoming an entrepreneur, remember that it's going to take time; primarily time necessary for you to practice this new skill.

Encourage yourself with the thoughts you permit to enter your mind and the words you forge with your tongue and permit to pass your lips. Try incantations, that is repeating thoughts and ideas you want to etch on the record of your thought process and those that come to the forefront of your mind whenever you are faced with a situation that would usually bring up the old and stale scripts like 'I can't do it.' Repeat them continually, as you would with a set of push-ups. Do ten "I can do this" out loud and in a mirror, and take a sip of water. Try it now and see how good it makes you feel. 'I CAN DO THIS!' "Whatever I set my mind to do, I can achieve". Now try ten of these. Say them loud and with all the belief you can muster. "I have everything it takes to create an enterprise that will make a huge impact in the market."

When I was on a recent vacation in Costa Rica, I was playing beach volley ball with a motley crew of men, women and children from around the world who I had flex and scream "This is Sparta" every time they scored a point. Our team continued to win every game straight for ten games is a row against a new and rested team. And finally, I had to leave the court because I was exhausted.

In a *Success Magazine* article, Suze Orman who is the bestselling author of *The Money Class: Learn to Create Your New American Dream*, host of *The Suze Orman Show* on CNBC, a two-time Emmy winner for her PBS specials and who *Forbes* has named as one of the ten most influential celebrities in the world, explains how she used affirmations to recreate her story and thought process.

Write a new truth that is the opposite of your greatest fear, she recommends. So if you are concerned about money, your new truth will be, "I have more money then I'll ever need". Then every day, she would write her new truth 25 times. She yelled it out loud 25 times and repeated it 25 times more while looking in a mirror.

Something to think about: *As the yoke to the pilot is the spoken word to the dreamer; each steering towards her ultimate destination.*

Chapter 7

Perception is Reality

"'Two men look out through the same bars; One sees the mud, and the other the starts."— Frederick Langbridge

In 1482, when Christopher Columbus boarded one of his three ships and got ready to sail, most of his crew had a perception of the world that was very different than the one we hold today. Many, if not all, thought that the earth was a flat disc, the ocean full of monsters capable of swallowing the ship whole and that, eventually, instead of discovering a new land with mountains of glittering gold and treasure, they would fall off earth's edge into a fiery abyss.

That perception was something that was very real in the minds of the people living during that time. It was the context to how they acted, felt, thought and what they would, ultimately, be willing to attempt.

It was only a perception of reality, but that fact made it no less real for those brave souls getting aboard that ship.

Our perceptions are very powerful and, once the right set of circumstances are created, people will behave in a way they would not otherwise.

Let's Play Doctor

A couple of friends of ours—let's call them Bill and Amy—were invited by an older couple from their congregation to their home for dinner. Around that time, Amy was very concerned about a lump she recently discovered. Knowing that her host was a physician, she decided to seek some advice. "Excuse me," she said quietly when they were alone. "I found a lump in my breast and was wondering if you wouldn't mind taking a look." He seemed a bit uncomfortable by the suggestion but graciously agreed. So Amy removes her blouse, unstraps her bra and guides his hand to the area of concern. By the expression on his face, he definitely felt something. After thinking about it for a minute, he said, "You know, we should probably have my wife take a look. She's the doctor."

So if the way we perceive our surroundings gets us to behave consistently with the beliefs we ultimately form in our mind, then we can say (with some confidence) that perception, for all intents and purposes, is reality.

Sorry. We Can't Help You

A young man in his early 20's was walking down a busy street during the morning rush. He looked fairly average—jeans, sneakers, jacket and a beanie hat. All of a sudden, he became visibly distressed, slowing his walk, coughing, holding his stomach as if in pain and slowly collapsing to the ground. There were lots of people walking by on their way to work, but no one stopped. It was as if nothing out of the ordinary happened. A man collapsed on the street in front of a crowd of people and not one person expressed any concern. Thankfully, the man was fine. He and his team were conducting a social experiment on how people react to the outward image we project. There he lay on that street for some five minutes as he tried to get the attention of those who passed by with "Excuse me, could you please help?" He had no luck. At one point, an elderly woman saw this man lying there on the concrete floor purportedly in pain, looked over in his direction and then just kept on going wherever she was headed originally.

Later, they repeated the experiment, but this time, that same man was dressed in a suit and tie. Again he went through the same script; first he began coughing, then held his stomach as if in pain, and slowly collapsed to the ground. This time, however, the reaction from the passersby was instantaneous. People dropped what they were doing and ran over to help. "Sir, are you ok? Can you hear me?" they asked, visibly concerned.

You may say that it is unfair that people would behave that way just because of appearance. Here they are rushing over to save a man in a suit and allowing one who is dressed plainly to die at their feet. But in defense of the human race, I'd just like to say that we have all been taken advantage of. Our kindness and humanity was used as a tool to leverage the self-interest of some predator looking out solely for his own interests. So as the years pass by, we try to create some kind of protective shell, using our mind to quickly ascertain a situation based on short cuts and decide the best course of action. Anything else would be considered credulous.

A Wrinkled House

When I try to explain to professionals how important their image is and that they should invest in quality clothing so as to ameliorate their appearance, sometimes it's a tough sell. Once this innocuous suggestion became a virtual debate as the doctor I was speaking with offered up the ornery, patient-loathing Gregory House, MD who is never shaved and usually sporting a mismatched outfit with a wrinkled shirt. Although I must admit that I like the show and have been watching the diagnostic, life-saving miracles of this fictional character for some time, I have to remind myself that everything is possible with the magic of television.

Considered the best diagnostician in the world, he and his team are besieged with complex and interesting cases that they usually solve like some version of the Teraminx Rubik's cube. But what would happen if we put Dr. House in his own practice with all the nuances of entrepreneurship? Would he be able to thrive as he does in the context of one of the larger and more prestigious institutions where he supposedly works currently? Personally, I have my doubts because usually those who tend to be very skilled in their craft are virtually impatient when it comes to the practicalities of self-employment.

To that point, J. Paul Getty (once considered the wealthiest man in the world) said, "I'd rather try to make a good technician out of a good executive who has no technical knowledge than try to make a good executive out of a good technician who has no executive ability."

It becomes very difficult for a doctor to realize that she is no longer this professional expert but now she is the marketing representative of this expert. She is not in the business of wellness but in the business of marketing wellness. She goes from being a gear in a large machine to now being the machine, itself, albeit much smaller.

If you could look like a roustabout in the polished halls of a large established enterprise, it becomes very different when the background changes, like on the stage of a high-budget Broadway show and all you have is a few newly-painted walls and your framed diploma.

Having worked with, marketed and interviewed some of the top physicians from around the world, there is a distinct difference in appearance with those considered "the best". Usually they look the part and would fit nicely on the cover of GQ or some other fashion publication.

Think about a police woman and the authority her uniform demands. What if we put her in a ballerina outfit with a pink tutu? And even if she still had the gun, would her presence carry the same weight? What if our financial advisor was wearing a shirt that was frayed at the cuffs or the suit jacket worn at the elbows? What if the keynote speaker wore pants that were so short they revealed his socks, reminding of the dorky Steve Urkel from *Family Matters*, as he tried to motivate us from the stage? Would we be able to focus on his message? How about if the chef who prepared the magnificent dish you were enjoying came out to greet you and you noticed dirt under his fingernails? Or cat hair on his clothes? What would those seemingly unimportant things communicate?

Once I went to see a medical doctor who specialized in weight loss. When I walked into his office, I was surprised to see that the man was not just overweight, he was obese. I was there trying to discuss business and was not looking for his professional services, but that image stayed with me. If I wanted to lose weight, get healthy, grow hair or become rich would I want to go to someone like him or a professional who actually looks the part?

There is an unflattering word that applies to those who preach one message but live their life in complete contradiction. They tell us how to live but they, themselves, do the opposite, as evidenced by their very presence.

We can, perhaps, debate which came first, the image of success or success itself, but (usually) the right image helps it along very nicely. It's the difference between being on a sailboat during a windy day and carrying a panel of sheetrock. With one, you can set your sails to move you in the direction you wish to go, and with the other, you'll flail around at the mercy of the wind.

The Clown Will See You Now

Spending a few days in Anaheim, California, I was attending one of the larger natural product expos in the world. As I was making my way through some of the endless isles of exhibits separated by pipe and drape, I noticed a familiar face. He was dressed in colorful baggy pants, a red shirt and a yellow tie. He had long, gray hair that was parted down the middle, colored purple on one side and tied in a ponytail that ran down his back, passed the belt, just reaching his coccyx. He sported a hanging earring on his left ear and a red ball on his nose just above a gray, handle-bar mustache. His name is Patch Adams, a medical doctor and the inspiration to a very fun movie where his life was portrayed by Robin Williams. He is also the founder of a holistic hospital called The Gesundheit Institute in West Virginia.

He was there standing near a booth of some supplement company and interacting with the people who stopped to take a photo with him. The only prerequisite for the photo-op, was that you had to do it with your finger inserted in your nose as he did the same with his.

I like Patch. He is an idealist who believes that medical care is a right and that everyone should be able to have access to it without cost. His doctors are paid a $300-per-month stipend with a waiting list of candidates who apply regularly to live and work in his center. To support his hospital model, he and his original medical team worked full time jobs and financed the entire project with no outside help. It's noble—and I think necessary—although not very practical and hardly a scalable endeavor.

But since we are on the topic of perception and reality; if you choose to give-away your highly valued services for free and Hollywood makes a blockbuster movie about your life, I think you can look pretty much however you like.

Here's a Power Point

At one time in my life, I apprenticed as a jeweler. One side of my family is pretty established in that industry and a few have done exceptionally well. It was interesting work, although one would spend their days sitting in front of a work bench with tiny tools, hand saws and welding equipment. My job was mostly to polish the newly-cast rings and file out the imperfections before stones were set as the ring would make its way into the glass showcase.

My cousin who had spent his entire life in that field and was considered very talented in both the designs he created and pieces that he would actually fashion, once decided that he wanted to apply for a job at Tiffany's, one of the oldest and most prestigious jewelry retailers in the world.

They granted an interview, and he had to prep a ring for them to examine his abilities, and determine whether he would qualify to work there. He spent the day diligently working on a sample to present and, finally, submitted an impressive piece that would surely curry favor with those making the hiring decision.

At first, the three judges looked over the ring with their naked eye. Then they examined it with a jeweler's magnifying glass that they held with the socket of their dominant eye. All seemed well until, finally, they placed the ring in front of a projector throwing the shadow-image onto a large white screen. It was there, on a wall in front of them, that his fate was sealed. The enormous, black image on a large, white canvas clearly showed what seemed like a million blatant imperfections; evidence that, as good as he was, he was not ready to play at this level of excellence.

So it is with us who aspire to make our mark on the world, and hunger that our chance would come quicker then it usually does. The larger the fame and the bigger the fortune, the more glaring our imperfections become. So it is wise to use the time before we find ourselves projected onto the large, white screen on the large world stage, that we make every effort to diligently create a polish that will best permit us to take advantage of the opportunity when it, inevitably, presents itself.

You Need Your Head Shot

When I first began marketing integrative doctors, I would ask them to send me a headshot so I could use it in my printed or digital promotional materials. It struck me as peculiar that the response I received was "I don't really have a headshot," or they would send me a photo where someone they were hugging was cropped out or they were wearing V-neck scrubs, exposing a thick patch of chest hair. I've seen shots of some of my lady doctors that would have been nice for a Victoria's Secret catalogue or perhaps *Wine & Spirits* or *Imbibe Magazine* since they were in a bar holding a drink.

But if a picture says a thousand words, then what does a bad one say?

With all the different digital platforms available today that require a headshot, it is imperative—in my mind—that we put our best foot forward, sota' speak. There are so many ways that an upper-torso photo can be used to communicate a message of professionalism, attention to detail, quality and a particular niche. A chef can be working on a beautiful dish, a cardiologist can hold a plastic anatomic heart model, an ophthalmologist can stand near some interesting piece of eye testing equipment, and of course a holistic gynecologist can just look thoughtfully past the camera.

Take One: Overture.

Some of the professionals I work with, those who choose to open an integrative practice of their own, really give very little thought to what I think are critically important aspects of a new enterprise, specifically the ability for people to reach you when needed. Some still don't check their email or the voice mail on their cell phone. Many don't set up a greeting, and when you are told to leave a message, it's by some automated voice that makes you wonder if you reached the correct number. Some only communicate through Facebook and others only through texting. Some still don't have business cards. And many (if they do reply to your email) don't have an email signature, nor address you by name in the communication; you know, that sound that Dale Carnegie, the renowned author of *How To Win Friends and Influence People*, calls the sweetest, most important sound in any language.

When I worked with Dr. Linchitz, this man spoiled me with his ability to communicate and engage on all platforms and do it, relatively, instantaneously. He always returned calls the same day and emails within a few hours. He corresponded with patients on Facebook and always, somehow, was able to find time for people who needed him. In essence, he was not only very approachable, but also very reachable.

In the early stages of our relationship, I would call him with different ideas and suggestions and he would always take the time to answer, even if the answer was not what I was hoping to hear. His engagement was reassuring and endearing. Over time, once we got on the same page, I had a better sense of how he thought and what he wanted, so although I had his cell phone on speed dial and his email at my fingertips, I only used them when absolutely necessary. Knowing that he was always there when I needed him, however, created a bond and a level of trust that took my effort and passion for spreading his message way beyond the client / provider relationship. I imagine his many patients felt the same way.

One very powerful marketing tool that costs absolutely nothing is the email signature. It is a clue, for those with whom we communicate, about who you are on a level deeper than just name and creds. My email signature, for example, has all of my contact information, links to my website, one to a pertinent article I wrote, and a quote that spells out my philosophy. Recently, I added the piece de résistance: an Overture video. You can see it if you like at overture.me/alexlubarsky

Jared Matthew Weiss is one of the more interesting people I have met in my life. He is also the founder of a company that produces short videos that aim (in just 30 seconds) to bring out your true self. It's called "Overture". Jared's mission is to help people around the world get to know each other. And since we will usually do business (at least the kind of intimate business that is healing) with people we like, trust and believe will help us, there are few things digitally as powerful as these well-thought-out, and professionally directed, little windows into your deeper self and the mystery that is you.

So what I'm saying is that it is vital to first look the part and then showcase this polished image using professional platforms that best capture and communicate it. We want to make ourselves easily reachable; and something interesting about who we are and what we do, easily sharable.

Alex Lubarsky

The Earth Is Flat, But So Is Health Care

In a few generations, when our great-grandchildren study our culture through fossils, time capsules and hard drives, one of the things that will surely get them to scratch their head in bewilderment will be our health as a nation and the system we created to address it. Perhaps like those sailors of old who set out to discover a new world and the treasures they hoped were there, we have a set of paradigms through which we see our system of care and think that it is reality, when it's nothing more than a waterfall in the desert—in other words . . . a mirage. It is the modern version of monsters in the ocean and the fiery abyss at earth's edge. It is what we know and accept as our tangible reality.

But how should our health care be structured and how would we explain the current system of care to a group of five-year-olds?

"Well, children, the doctors will work for the ever-expanding hospital system, mill through as many patients as possible on a daily basis, identify and label their disease and prescribe a medication to suppress the symptoms."

"Sure. Okay. That makes sense."

"Who should pay for the services the doctor renders?"

"It should be paid by a third party; one that has nothing to do with providing care, like an insurance company, the government or maybe the monks of Tibet."

"Why, yes, of course. Why not monks?"

148

"And who should pay for the insurance policy that the patient brings to the doctor?"

"Most definitely, it has to be the employer, you know; those of us who go to work and get paid in insurance, time off and paper clips."

"Yea. That's obvious."

"So what happens if you get paid in cash and not in insurance or office supplies and need to go see a doctor. What do you do then?"

That's easy. We'll just get all the people who like to work to chip in and pay for those who don't have the means to pay for a doctor visit just now. So then, the great modern healer can perform a medical version of a 'quickie'; identify and label their disease and prescribe some medication to temporarily suppress the symptoms.

"Perfect. Let's go with that."

"Excuse me. What if we focus at least a part of our resources on wellness, prevention and addressing the underlying causes through education and life-style-management?"

"What?! . . . That is a stupid question. Please take your things and leave the room."

So, let me just get this straight. The average person will make every effort to daily undermine their health because they don't know how to eat and nourish their body, they don't understand how important physical activity is for their health and vitality, and their environment

---

is toxic (they microwave processed meat in a Styrofoam container, allowing the hormone-altering chemicals to permeate the dead nutrient-zero substance barely resembling foodstuffs). And then we are going to centralize care so that it will be provided to everyone for free by an all-knowing- bureaucracy from the very top?

Yes. Yes we are.

Our modern day health care system is a hodge-podge of emotion, fear and ignorance. It has been politicized, emotionalized and entangled in over 65 years of antiquated policy, moldy laws and stale territorial systems of control. It has become some version of a business that's too big to fail and too obstinate to change, so like the sprouts from a handful of magic beans planted a long time ago, it's growing out of control and will only stop when it collapses from its own weight. Kind of like the USSR.

I think that every so often we have to sit down and re-examine the things and institutions we have accepted as infallible. What was a great idea during the great depression may no longer be practical in the current reality.

Certainly in today's world, we have seen more change in just a few years than a person would have been exposed to their entire life. Almost daily we see men and women, no different than you or I, transform entrenched industries, making old ways of doing and thinking obsolete virtually overnight. We know that where there was only computers, there is now the World Wide Web, where there was only man-driven cars, today there are one's that drive themselves, and where there was only NASA, now Virgin Galactic is offering space tourism. Indeed

150

these are exciting, and fast moving times, for those riding the crest of the wave and very unpleasant and frightening ones for those swimming beneath it.

I'm a Doctor, Not a Forklift

In the area where I live, there is a doctor who has branded himself as the "weight-loss MD", and that is the message (emblazed on the back cover of a local *Pennysaver* throwaway) that every so often gets shoved through the mail slot of my front door. But the word "doctor" in Latin means "teacher" not "advertiser". So even if he does get some patients out of this misguided effort, I think it's a demeaning way of prostrating professional services.

If, on the other hand, I was selling a forklift, this would probably be as good a venue as any to let people know that I have it and you can buy it from me if you like. It's a tangible item, not unlike shampoo, a watch, or a set of Ginsu knives that you can buy right now, today, because there won't be any more tomorrow or ever.

But wait, there's more.

Although some have claimed that I can sell ice to Eskimos, I have never sold anything to anyone. Ever. Selling something implies that they did not want to buy and I strong-armed them into the purchase. Kind of like a sleazy salesman who once came into my shop when I was still a pup. He used every technique in the book to sell me on some useless advertising that I knew would prove to be fruitless. He came over to my side of the counter, assumed the sale, got me to nod along with him as he asked closed-ended questions while filling out the contract and then, handing me his pen, as he pointed to the big red X. That is not selling. It's manipulation of the worse kind. And it did not take me long to get very good at identifying and resisting those dubious tactics and people.

What I do is first try to clearly identify what someone needs or is looking to accomplish, and then I work my tail to the bone (and my mind till it begins to smoke, if ever so slightly) to help provide the very best possibilities so as to assure the achievement of that thing which they said they want to achieve. In essence, I don't sell, but I do try very hard to help people buy. Also, I consider it my job to encourage people through some of the difficult times when they may want to quit because the results have not caught up with the effort as quickly as they may have liked. I try to remind my clients of their original objective and help get them past the fear and doubt to where they can better see their goals coming to fruition.

So what we've become fairly proficient at doing at Health Media, is positioning our doctors as experts and teachers in their particular modality, approach or niche. Then we market and sell their appearance at an event, where they share valuable information with those who attend. And then we videotape a part of their lecture and market the video as far as resources permit, but usually (to the bewilderment of our accountant) slightly beyond. We sell an opportunity to improve one's life through transformational information and the people who provide it. We don't, however, sell the doctor like a pack of #2 pencils.

It's Not You. It's Her

We usually hold our events at one of the Hilton family of upscale hotels. Although we could probably save many thousands of dollars by using a school gymnasium or a room in some of the houses of worship where I've attended other events, I've always felt that the context of the venue either contributes to the professional image we want to communicate or takes away from it. So the extra that it costs to use the higher quality location is more than offset by the credibility it brings to the event and the people who are a part of it.

So the environment we create around us, and the people who we have represent us, are a direct extension of our image and, therefore, demand our most rigorous attention. They are not part of our organization, they are the organization, itself; a direct connection that no client will bother to distinguish when they complain that the service was terrible, or people inept.

"Yes, may I help you?" the woman answered when I called the dealership where I recently purchased a minivan that I needed to chauffeur my street team as we promoted an upcoming event.

"Hi. I'm looking for someone who can help me wrap the vehicle I just purchased from you."

"You want to do what?"

"You know, place promotional graphics on the van I just bought. I was told you offer that service."

"Hold on," she said as I was placed on a ten-minute hold.

"Hello."

"Yes."

"Who is this?"

"I was calling about the graphics for my car."

"Who's calling?"

"Alex Lubarsky."

"What? I'm sorry. We don't have anyone by that name."

"Aha. Any chance I can speak with the manager?" . . .

Even if this was a case of nepotism (where someone was obligated to hire a relative) or just a poor hiring choice, matters little; because 'Abbot' is doing untold damage to this business and its image with her unprofessional 'Who's on First' routine and impersonal demeanor. The person who is the first point of contact (and the one who will, ultimately, set the tone for the entire client experience) has to be well-trained and should, preferably, be someone who enjoys dealing with people and knows how to speak to them.

Knowing Is Not Doing

If we were to ask the average person on the street if they know how to lose weight, I am sure that most people will tell us that all you have to do is eat well and exercise. And mostly, they would be right. So if most of us know how to do it, why is it that, as a nation, we are becoming more overweight from one year to the next even though we are spending billions on weight-loss products and services? And if we were to ask those same people about the best way to approach finances, they would most likely (and fairly accurately) offer that we should live within our means and save a percentage to invest or put away for a rainy day. So why is it that so many people live beyond their means and have virtually no savings?

Just because we know how to do something does not mean we are going to do it. And the reasons for that could be many and fairly complex. Maybe we're trying to feed some childish emotion, or we simply get so busy we forget, or everyone around us is living the same way so we just kind of accept that since everyone is doing it. It's probably acceptable for us, as well.

So after years of trial and error, I no longer ask my clients to provide me with headshots or write articles. I simply created the infrastructure to make sure I get everything I need to fashion the image that will be most effective as quickly as possible. So we've hired a number of photographers who we send to our new clients. I have a team of writers who help craft the message of the people we are promoting. We have graphic designers and even a bespoke clothing group that we'll engage so as to make sure that we get what we need quickly and with as little distraction as possible.

So all our client has to do is make a decision that they will commit to about 24 months with us and we do, virtually, all the rest. This way, with minimal effort or thought about marketing, they begin moving in the direction they envision for themselves and their practice while maintaining their focus where it's most needed—on their patients. It's kind of like when Iron Man suits up. Tony Stark just presses a button and all the robotic machines kick in and begin to dress him in his suit of high-tech armor. It just happens automatically, and once it's done, he takes off to save the world. And so it is.

Something to think about: *In water we swim, in air we fly, on the ground we walk, and in fire we burn. Thus it's the context where we find ourselves that fosters the actions we take and the destiny we reap.*

Chapter 8

It Has to Be Youuuu

"In a gentle way, you can shake the world." — Mahatma Gandhi

When people ask me what I do for a living, I usually answer, "I am transforming health care in America." Of course, there is no way for me to know that I will ever do anything more than produce a few events and give out some flyers. But having this tremendously huge purpose for my life illuminates everything I do each and every day. Somehow, it puts more energy and motivation in my every interaction. It guides my thoughts, brings a level of confidence to my decision-making process, and ignites creativity beyond the realm of what I may have believed possible.

And . . . what if?

What if I was actually the one who somehow influenced the way we do health in this nation? Put a dent in that universe, if you will. Wouldn't that be awesome? So regardless of fact, or what anyone may think of me or my ideas, that is how I'm going to play this game. And I invite you to play at that same level as well. Because would it not be terrible if we get to the end of our life knowing that we could have done so much more, indeed, could have become so much more. Even worse, through our inaction, we permit self-serving and destructive forces to flourish as we "the good people" quietly sit by and watch it happen.

You Don't Need to Turn Green to Make a Difference

I still did not speak or understand English when I first saw Dr. David Bruce Banner, the man who, inadvertently, exposed himself to the radiation of the Gamma Transponder (a device he helped create) that transformed him from a geeky, introverted scientist into a green, super-strong and very muscular creature every time he became angry. Looking back, I think the Hulk enjoyed such popularity because it connected with our innate belief that there is something in each of us that would allow us to do those things we envision in our mind if we did not immediately suppress them, because we see the big flashing sign that says "UNREALISTIC".

We've all heard stories of people performing unbelievable feats of strength or ability when properly motivated, like a mother who lifts a car off her child or a man who jumps a ten-foot-wall when chased by a tiger. When asked to repeat their hard-to-believe claim later they (of course) could not do it. But if one person can do something remarkable in a certain situation, then it stands to reason that, with the right set of circumstances and the right motivation, we all can.

So what would be the "final-straw -condition" that would allow you to tap those reserve, Hulk-like powered abilities and propel you out of a world, inadvertently, created for you by your environment (a world that you were born into and have had little or nothing to say about) into one of your own design? How do we get our feet out of the mud of average mediocrity, spread our wings and take flight into the extraordinary?

An Army of One

Josh Umbehr is the founder of Atlas MD in Wichita, Kansas. He is a medical doctor who was watching those who graduated medical school just a few years before him get completely burned out trying to function in the current bureaucratic model of care. So when he finally received his diploma from the Kansas University School of Medicine and became board certified as a family doctor, he knew that following the white coat-wearing herd was not what he wanted to do. Taking a big gamble, he decided to re-imagine health care and approach it from a very different angle.

His dad began his working life in the trash business. So early on, Josh learned the value of hard work and personal responsibility. He did not mind long hours or getting his hands dirty. Later, selling his business, Umbehr Sr. went back to school and earned his law degree, becoming successful in that field as well and inspiring his children to pursue more cerebral endeavors.

Having a natural interest and aptitude in science, Josh decided to become a doctor. As soon as he received his medical degree, however, it was kind of like getting off the plane and entering the lugubrious world of George Orwell's *Nineteen Eighty-Four; a* grey and depressing, over-regulated, government-controlled and stifling system of red tape, bureaucracy and draconian oversight where innovation was frowned upon, creativity discouraged and doctors turned into some version of Walter (that grouchy, cynical hand puppet animated by the famous humorist Jeff Dunham), in that case, and the federal government in this one.

In four short years, however, Atlas MD and Dr. Umbehr are thriving. Not only from a practical business point of view, but also from the freedom, satisfaction and actually enjoying-the-practice-of medicine one as well. Structuring his business model resembling a gym or Netflix membership, each of his 600 or so patients pays a monthly fee and enjoys concierge, time generous and instantaneous care. Today, the practice has a total of three doctors and some 1500 member / patients.

In our interview, Dr. Umbehr mentioned a quote: "If you want something done, don't ask the man familiar with the task and knows it cannot be done. Ask the man who does not know that it cannot be done and he will do it." Certainly I agree with that. But what about if you and I are that man who knows that it cannot be done? What if we were taught, and have seen enough evidence to support the belief, that it cannot be done. Are we just destined to not do it? Are we then fated to be held prisoner by a limiting belief? For ever?

Doing the Impossible Will Take a Little Longer

On July 21, 2007, Allan Webb ran the mile in just a hair over 3 minutes 46 seconds. When asked if he had a message for those watching back home, he looked into the camera and said, "Dreams come true." The interesting thing was that Allan was able to say anything after such a grueling run. Back in 1954, Sir Roger Gilbert Bannister was the first person ever to break the four-minute mile at 3 minutes 59 seconds and collapsed into the arms of those waiting at the finish line. He was not able to say much of anything because he had just accomplished what everyone knew was impossible. It was not a physical limitation, for after he broke that invisible barrier, that year some 37 people did it as well. Today, everyone from junior to senior is doing it; in fact, my 96-year-old grandmother can do it while carrying a tray of freshly-baked cookies.

The only way Sir Bannister was able to do what was never done before, is he had to build enough evidence around him to support that belief. He also needed a support system of people who created the perfect environment for that belief to grow into a conviction. Once there, breaking through that glass wall, was only a matter of time. He was the first to do the impossible because, in his mind, he had already done it a thousand times.

Henry Ford said that whether you think you can or you think you can't, you're right. And once we've seen someone do what we were sure could not be done, at least now we are willing to open our mind to possibility and maybe try it as well. In the case of Dr. Umbehr and his partner Dr. Nunamaker, for all intents and purposes, they have broken the barrier that said you need to participate with insurance to have a medical practice, you have to accept government programs to succeed, and you have to prostrate your talents and hard-earned abilities to survive in the modern Lenin-esque system of care.

Through their example, perhaps many other physicians will break through their own mental four-minute mile and give the free market a try. And even if one man cannot make all the difference on his own, he or she can ignite the fire of possibility in others, creating a cascade that transforms everything. So on the other hand, maybe he can. Maybe you can.

As the artificial tsunami of government-imposed, compulsory care begins to recede, it inadvertently created the perfect and fertile environment for market-driven centers like Atlas MD to bloom.

The Road to Good Intentions

There is a wide chasm between the birth of an idea in the mind of its creator and that place where profits begin to overtake expenses. It is a process that takes time to understand and implement. There are laws that need to be understood and followed, and consequences dealt with when they are ignored.

When I was first learning how to drive a car, there were those obvious laws that I learned to follow fairly early on: Like stop on a red light, drive on the right side of the street when in the United States and most civilized countries of the world, yield to pedestrians, use your signals, when on a one-way street, drive in the direction of all the other cars, and wear your seatbelt. That last one was encouraged by six different police officers who insisted that it was a good idea. But here is one I learned myself; after the light turns green, take a second before you take off, maybe even glance around, especially at a major intersection. Believe me when I tell you that this little known law has saved me some potentially very unpleasant moments, as well as the fellow who flew his black truck with way too much chrome past my nose a full two seconds after my light said, "go".

The main purpose of any marketing effort it to grow your business. That's all and nothing else. This is an important law to consider before we agree to hand over our hard-earned resources to someone proposing to build brand awareness. When I spend a dollar on marketing, I expect to get more than a dollar back. If my effort does not produce that kind of a result, something needs fixin'. So now we have to inspect the entire assembly line and figure out where the break down is. Is the message resonating with the audience we are reaching through the venue we chose? Is the offer compelling enough for them to consider the service being offered? Am I aiming my message at the right demographic? Is my image consistent with the message I'm trying to communicate? Am I reaching enough people to identify those who are primed to make a decision right now? Are they seeing my message? Do they understand it? Does anyone answer the phone should a potential client dial my office number to ask a question? Am I easily reachable? And finally, who is my best client?

There are plenty other laws one can learn fairly easily as we take off towards our goal and begin gaining more experience. We can learn those laws from reading instruction manuals in the form of books. We can learn them by attending seminars, and we can learn them by evaluating our daily experiences and pealing a few layers to learn the lessons they hold.

If Not You, Who?

If you saw a two-year-old girl who was just hit by a car lying on the street unconscious, what would you do? Would you call for help? Would you lift her in your arms, put her in your car and drive her to the nearest emergency room? Or would you just walk by, pretending that you did not notice?

It is a harsh picture I know, but it is also a practical one. It seems that in Foshan, China, a little girl was hit by a van and then hit again by another vehicle as she played on the street near her dad's store. She lay on the street for some 10 minutes as dozens of people walked by sidestepping her unconscious body as if nothing unusual was going on.

Sure, that is a possible scenario in a place like China. With over a billion people, a quickly developing economy and a historic preference of boys over girls, where the latter were simply abandoned, or more recently, terminated using sex selective abortions, when identified though modern technology.

Something like this could never happen in the United States where life is sacred and we have been brought up under the Judeo-Christian "do unto others'" philosophy.

On her way home after working late as a bar manager, Catherine Susan Genovese, a 28-year-old woman was brutally attacked, stabbed multiple times and raped over a period of over 30 minutes as many of her neighbors in a densely-populated community of a New York borough, looked on. Originally, it was said that some 37 people were watching the attack take place from their windows and no one called for or offered help. "Kitty" as she was known, succumbed to her injuries on the way to the hospital, when someone finally called the police, long after the perpetrator ran off with the $49 he stole from her purse.

Sixteen Dripping Candles

We were at the party of one of our friends' daughters who was celebrating her birthday in the catering hall of a Russian restaurant in Brooklyn. There were about 200 of us seated behind some 20 round tables set up in a horseshoe formation around the dance floor and stage up front.

She was holding a ten-inch long candle in her right hand, using it to light the other 16 set up in front of her as she read from the notes she was holding in her left, honoring some of the family and friends who would come up and take pictures with our lovely guest of honor as their names were called.

There was a photographer taking pictures, the master of ceremonies who was leading the festivities, a video crew capturing the occasion on film and all of us enjoying the moment as we watched it unfold.

The lit candle that she was holding began to drip and as the hot wax fell onto the skin of her hand she would make a slight grimace and under her nose voice "ouch" each time it would happen. We were all there, we all saw this happening right in front of us; and yet no one did anything about it. It was interesting to watch, because we knew most of the people who were there. They would all give you the shirt off their back. They were kind, thoughtful and many were leaders in their fields. But no one did anything to rectify what was clearly a situation that needed attention. After what seemed like forever, one of the guests finally got up, took his white cloth napkin and wrapped it around the bottom of the candle, handing it back to a grateful birthday girl and relieving some palpable anxiety in the room.

Hypnosis by Masses

Perhaps we should not be too hard on ourselves though. As humans, there are certain features that come standard on every model and are hard wired, deep into the neurotransmitters of our mind. If you and I were in a baseball stadium in the middle of a well-attended game, for example, and someone jumped out of their seat, began to scream and run for the exit. What would you do? In most probability, you would glance over at the commotion and continue watching the game. But now, what if everyone in the stadium jumped out of their seat, started screaming and ran for the door? What would you do then? Now, I think you and I would be tripping over each other trying to get out. Why? Did we see anything to get us to act in lock step with the frenzied masses? Not necessarily. We just assume how most people behave around us must make it the correct way to behave. For the mindless crowd knows best.

What was supposed to be a humorous video became a social experiment of sorts; one that very clearly illustrates how the people around us have an uncanny ability to cause us to act illogically—just because everyone else is acting that way.

As a person was walking down a street, a group of about 25 average-looking antagonists turned behind them walking at an accelerated pace. As the group began passing their unsuspecting victim, the leader yelled, "*Duck!*" and the entire group fell to the ground, covering their heads with their hands. Since the person who was now, unknowingly, in the middle of this staged event and could only see what was happening around them, taking their clues from the crowd, they also abruptly fell to the ground. After a few seconds of this, the leader got up and gave the next order: "*Run!* Again, as the crowd took off, so did it's now-hypnotized-by-the-masses subject. They repeated this "experiment" over and over, generating uproarious laughs from the audience later watching the video. Each of the subjects behaved in now a predictable fashion, exactly as the group around them. They ducked when everyone ducked and they ran when everyone ran even though there was no practical reason for it.

Perhaps at one time in our history, it was helpful to run when you saw a group running because chances are that, at any moment, a carnivorous dinosaur was about to turn the corner and seriously disrupt your schedule. Today, I think it's much less helpful because, clearly, there are those who figured out that this is a human default mechanism and use it against us with abandon. Or worse, we use it against ourselves. The only way for us to avoid being manipulated in this way is to take a step back and realize that we are susceptible to such influences. By recognizing its existence, it can no longer hold us prisoner. Sort of like a child who gets up enough courage to get out of bed in the dark, walk over to the open closet in their room and confront the monster with the glowing eyes. Once he sees that it is only his jacket that resembled the face of Bigfoot in the darkness with the shiny buttons reflecting the green LED light of the electric clock on his desk, he can release the fear and gain a strategic advantage over his environment and life.

You Got Who Running Health Care?

Let's imagine for a moment that you and I lived on a deserted island and in a community of ten people. You were the captain of our little canoe and I was your second mate. Our job was to fish for the community. There was a healer, a builder, professor, a cook, an elder and a fool who spent his days on the roof of one of the huts moving the sun across the sky. Everyone did their job and even though the elder was not able to work because of his age and the fool because he was concerned with grander projects, the ecosystem of the community worked.

One day during a storm, our little vessel was thrown out to sea and, after a week of thirst and hunger, ended up in proximity to the Florida pan handle. When we stepped foot on to the United States soil and got a look at this civilized society, what would be some of the thoughts running through our mind?

First, we would notice all the overweight children, the multitudes of adults dealing with some kind of chronic disease and the mountains of medications that we consumed as a society. And, that the fool is in charge of health care. Well how else would you explain that when the builder goes to see the healer, the professor, the cook and you send fish to the guy busy moving the sun across the sky, he eats up most of it and sends the tail and bones to the doctor? Since the doctor can only survive by seeing way too many patients every day, he can barely afford a few minutes for each interaction, usually ending the visit with a prescription for another symptom-suppressing medication.

"Why doesn't the builder just give the fish to the healer directly?" we would ask each other. Does not that make more sense? Wouldn't the doctor be able to see less people on a given day and, therefore, allocate more time to each so that, perhaps, she can uncover the underlying problems and actually heal her patient while reducing our addiction on medication? At the same time, since she's thriving, she volunteers her time to educate children about nutrition and fitness and donates a day a week (and a week a year) to working with those who cannot afford care, because she wants to. And now she can invest her disposable income in industries that she believes in—like wellness.

Sure it does.

In fact, if we really wanted to accomplish universal access to care, all we have to do is make seeing people who can't afford to pay a doctor tax deductible.

This is a much more likely scenario than the politician who is going to collect money from all the citizens based on ability and then, equally and fairly, divide that pile of cash based on need. But the hypnotized masses are looking at this convoluted system and don't see anything wrong with it. In fact, when they try to fix it because it clearly is not working, they try to do it by making it even more convoluted.

"Let's send more fish to the fool," they scream. The fishermen are not paying their fair share because they are being stingy and lazy. The healer is greedy because she is not satisfied with leftovers and scraps as payment. And the rest of society is "ducking" and "running" with everyone else, in spite of all evidence, reality or common sense.

Recently, I found myself driving behind a well-worn minivan and I was saddened to see that it had MD plates. This is not an aberration, but is a fairly common occurrence in the current reality. I remember a time when you saw MD plates they were attached to the kind of car you would want to aspire to own one day. So what exactly are we tacitly saying to the next generation?" Hey, kid. Go to school for like half your life, work hard, spend a fortune on education, get heavily in debt with student loans, and you'll make enough money to afford a car that no self-respecting plumber would be caught dead in."

The socialization of our health care system began in 1965 with the founding of Medicare which provides a free or subsidized government health insurance to our seniors. Now, we simply took it to the next natural step and put our entire society under that same plan. As the rest of the world is running away from socialism and government control, we are embracing it with both arms. Sure, perhaps, as the federal government continues to grow, it needs these kinds of programs to gain more control and generate more revenue to fund its insatiable gluttony. For you and me, however, it's a very different story. We want to be free. We don't want anyone controlling us, looking over our shoulder and questioning our integrity without cause. We want to be in charge of our own lives and deal freely with our fellow citizens. And we want to succeed to the highest levels that our talents, education, creativity and work ethic permit. Not that there's anything wrong with that.

Let "It" Go; For "It" Does Not Exist

It is difficult to contemplate change when you are already doing everything to stay the same. Most doctors are hanging on the edge of an imagined precipice, holding on with both hands and for dear life. And as they look up, they see three bureaucrats blocking the sun and most of the sky. One is the insurance company, the other is the government and the third is Vladimir Ilyich Lenin, representing everyone who feels entitled to free care.

All three are telling the doctor not to worry and that everything will be better soon if he just continues to follow their rules, as they conjure them up on the spot and to their benefit. They don't offer to help him up because they want him where he is, and everything they say and do is used to keep him in his place. They use his respect for authority, his penchant to follow the rules, his love for patients, and the actual practice of healing to make sure he neither pulls himself up nor let's go because, in either case, the illusion they created will evaporate like morning dew on a warm summer day. (Or, perhaps, a more accurate analogy would be: like yesterday's urine off a sweltering Manhattan sidewalk.)

Being an outsider, as I stand and watch this dramatic episode unfold, I have a glimpse of the event from a different angle and from some distance. It is perplexing to me because, from where I'm standing, I can see the doctor's feet are hanging just a few inches above the ground and if he would just let go, everything would change.

Your personal power, the thing that you can do and that no one can stop you from doing, is have some faith and let "it" go; because "it" does not exist. As more doctors untangle themselves from this smothering scheme of control, they will be free to create a system of care that serves the patient best, rewards the doctor accordingly and disbands every sinister gang of self-serving thugs who do nothing to contribute to that process.

Steve Jobs said it this way:

"When you grow up you tend to get told the world is the way it is and your life is just to live inside that world. Try not to bash into the walls too much, try to have a nice family, have fun and save a little money. That is a very limited life. Life can be much broader once you discover one simple fact, everything around you that you call life was made up by people that were no smarter than you, and you can change it, you can influence it, you can build your own things that other people can use. Once you learn that, you 'll never be the same again."

Amen, Brother Steve!

Alex Lubarsky

The Ugly Duckling Fallacy

There once was an ugly duckling that did not fit in with his family or anyone else for that matter. He was very sad and unhappy because no one liked him and everyone thought he was ugly. One day, he saw little white birds who looked just like him and who invited him to play with them. And when their mother swam up, he thought she was the most beautiful bird in the world. "You are not a duckling," she explained, "but a swan. And when you grow up, you will be the king of the pond."

It is a beautiful story that you probably heard as a child. But there are other stories that you carry around in your mind, and unlike this one that you know has been made up, you believe these stories to be true.

At a dinner date with a half dozen of our friends, I asked everyone to share what they think others thought of them. "How do you believe we perceive you?" - was my question. As we went around the table, it was interesting how some of the perceptions shared by those present did not match up with those we held about them. Even the spouse, in some instances, found the answer to be surprising because it did not align with the way they saw them, even though they were married for over two decades.

One of the guys there is generously over six-foot tall, handsome, Ivy-League-educated, has a beautiful family and is successful in business. He has traveled the world and hosts terrific affairs in his palatial home. At first, he tried to duck the question, sort of speak, but then when pressed he said that he is basically shy and that is how the world sees him. When I pointed out that it was simply a story he made up and one that has no basis in reality, he quickly shot me down and affirmed that he was, indeed, very shy.

We all have these fables that are the software of our thought process and what ultimately drives our emotions and actions. Mine could sound something like, "I am an immigrant who does not have formal education. English is my second language. I am too stupid to start a business. The best I can hope for is to be average. Success and happiness are for other people and not for me. I am not as good as all the smart, beautiful and gifted people around me. The rich get richer and the poor get poorer. It's not what you know, it's who you know. I can't spell and am terrified of public speaking."

Yours may be one of the following, "I can't sell. I'm not a business person. I don't understand marketing. I could never succeed being my own boss. I am not capable of starting an enterprise. I can't even spell 'entrepreneur'."

But all of these stories and many more like them are simply not true. They are made up and have no basis of fact, even though you and I spent years accumulating evidence to try and put some legs under this nebulous nonsense. We can just as easily identify them, let them go and create a more empowering story that supports our current mission and passion.

Avoiding the Chucky Syndrome

Looking Out for Number One, is the title of a book written by Robert J. Ringer in 1977; one that, according to the New York Times, became one of the top ten bestselling books of all time. Mothers and healers would find this idea of focusing on your own needs first abhorrent. Usually they put everyone else as a priority, selflessly serving those around them while giving little thought to their own needs. Our children, our patients, spouses, clients, our friends and all those people are counting on us. There's just not enough time left over for "number one". And if you've come thus far in this book, then I imagine you are at least a little like me: very passionate about what you are out to achieve and create in the world and are giving it everything you've got at the expense of everything you already have.

When the very pretty girl (who would later become my wife) came to the United States from Ukraine in the late 80's, she was seventeen years old. Since my Russian was limping and her English nonexistent, there was little we could discuss, so one of our fist dates were spent at the movies. My choice for cinematic excellence would have to take language into consideration so the movie I finally selected relied more on the visual then auditory. It was called *Chucky*, aka *The Lakeshore Strangler*.

In this masterpiece of classic movie-making, a Good Guy Doll is possessed by the spirit of a serial killer and, in some pretty gory scenes, goes around lashing out angrily, cutting up some gory scenes using a black-handled kitchen knife, and scaring the bejesus out of those of us who paid to see it.

Inside each of us, there is a child that resembles either the adorable Shirley Temple with her golden curls as she sings "On the Good Ship Lollypop" or maybe Gary Coleman, who played the charming and cheeky Arnold Jackson in *Different Strokes*, as he purses his lips and famously quips, "What'chu talkin' 'bout, Willis?" Each is innocent, kind, adorable and fun.

The trouble comes when you mistreat that child within. You make promises that you later break. You work them hard for extended periods of time, without giving them what they've been craving, and later demanding. So after years of this kind of abuse, they begin to rebel and turn into some version of Chucky. Well, how would you feel if I worked you with such intensity and then broke every promise I made to you, while putting you down and highlighting your imperfections at every opportunity? Some may call it burnout, but I call it the Chucky Syndrome . . . when that adorable little you within the adult you, turns into an angry, rebellious, bitter, tantrum-throwing, unproductive spawn of the devil.

So although I believe that one person can make all the difference, and I believe you may very well be she, I also think that it's important that you make provisions for the long road ahead and look out for number one . . . if only just a little.

Something to think about: *May you never get what you want at the price of what you already have.*

Chapter 9

Making Momentum out of Nothing At All

"We can complain because rose bushes have thorns, or rejoice because thorn bushes have roses."
— *Abraham Lincoln*

If you had the power of the Creator and were able to redesign how a tree comes into existence, would you do it differently? You could, for example, plant the tree as a very large toothpick that you would make appear in front of our eyes, stick it into the ground and then grow branches and roots as in a time lapse footage over a period of minutes. And if I and all the other mortals saw this new way of a tree manifestation, we would all think it a miracle.

But is it any less a miracle than when we place a tiny seed into dirt, give it a little sun, some water and time, and it grows into a beautiful, green, leafy factory, thousands of times its original size and weight, and one that turns carbon dioxide into life giving oxygen? And if the conditions are right, the seed will grow into the tree that is programmed within its DNA every time and without fail.

We are surrounded with such miracles every day, in every moment, in every interaction and experience. All we need do is focus our attention at everything that makes up our world to appreciate the level of abundance so generously bestowed on each of us. Yet most people are miserable in all of this wealth and destroy themselves trying to get someplace where they think they'll, ultimately, be happy, while at the same time undermining those very things along the way that have the ability to bring them all the health, wealth and happiness they could ever want.

We See What We Want to See

Ronald Regan loved to tell a story about twin boys. One was an awful pessimist and the other a hopeless optimist. One day, in an attempt to find out if they could get some optimism out of the pessimist, they put him in a room full of toys and games; and to get some pessimism out of the optimist, they put him in a room with a big pile of manure. When they came back a short time later, the pessimist was crying because one of the toys he was playing with broke. But when they came into the room where the optimist was, they were surprised to see him jumping on top of the pile of dung, laughing and throwing the smelly stuff all around the room. "Why are you so happy and excited?" they asked the boy covered in poop. "Well, with all this manure, there has to be a pony in here someplace," he answered.

We all know people who, no matter what happens around them, always focus on the problem. They never see any of the miracles, but only what's wrong. And that can make the wealthy poor because no matter how much they have, there is never enough. Even if you have a lot, it is still nothing compared to everything, so they are never happy or satisfied. On the other hand, someone who has little in worldly possessions but is grateful for what they have, and can only see the good and the positive as they go through life, are wealthy beyond measure.

Not to say it cannot be the other way around. There are plenty of wealthy people who are deeply grateful for each blessing they experience, and perhaps so many more of the poor who curse their lowly position and see nothing beyond it, as they resent and vilify anyone who is prospering. Assuring that they will never be able to have any more nor do any better, short of winning the lottery, which becomes their only tenuous thread of hope to ever get out of a life set in penurious mediocrity.

We can spend our days chasing our dreams and focusing on what we want, but at days end, it's imperative to give our attention to the people and things we already have and express our gratitude for them. This is also the foundation to building momentum in our endeavors; it is the fire that propels us forward.

Get Rich in the Great Depression

During one of the most difficult times in American history, unemployment reached some 25% and countless people spent their days either looking for scant work opportunities or in bars trying to wash away their sorrow. No matter how tough the economic situation may look today, or how uncertain the future may seem, I think we can come to some consensus that it was probably much more severe then, than it is today.

One of the companies I've had the pleasure of working with, and one who has supported our efforts from the very start, is a gourmet grocer called Wild by Nature. It is a terrific chain with five Long Island locations. Their shelves are stocked with everything organic, nutritious and gluten free, as well as thousands of other products with the health of the consumer in mind. They have a juice bar and a little restaurant on premises that also leans toward the more health-supporting options. One of the recent stores they built in Oceanside is LEED-certified, environmentally-friendly in its use of electricity, water and choice of materials in the construction of the building.

This smaller chain of stores is owned by King Kullen Supermarkets, which has about 52 locations throughout Long Island, New York, and that was founded by Michael J. Cullen on August 4, 1930. It has been recognized by the Smithsonian Institution as America's first supermarket, a fact that the chain uses as its tag line. This was probably not a good time to consider starting a business as it was the heart of the depression when countless enterprises were closing their doors and the economic situation seemed bleak with no end in sight. I am sure everyone told Mr. Cullen that his timing could not be worse and that his idea was foolhardy, to put it nicely.

And yet, in spite of all the criticism and the seemingly precarious reality of the moment, he was able to develop a tangible idea that catered to people's needs effectively and provided them with a valuable service at a reasonable price. So within six years, his small enterprise had grown to 17 stores and generated 6 million dollars in sales, a terrific sum in those years; and not too shabby today, either.

Blinded by the Light of Abundance

America is in a much better place than it has ever been. We have technological advances that are beyond comprehension, and yet so user-friendly, that two-year-olds are able to operate them with ease. Our economy, relatively speaking, is booming. We have access to the entire world and can easily do business from the comfort of our own home with anyone on the planet. The poorest among us have access to education, transportation, information, entertainment, food, clothing, and cell phones; those tiny computers that put, virtually, all the information of humanity at your fingertips. It is a miraculous time to be alive and anyone who wants to can succeed beyond measure. And yet, in the middle of all this abundance, the only thing most people can see is that one broken toy, or the thorns rather than the rose.

It is our focus that either makes us depressed when we are surrounded by abundance or inspired when we are in a room full of figurative manure. It is not reality, but our perception of it, that matters most, is what I'm trying to say.

You Must Have Been a Beautiful Baby

I was lucky enough to see both of my children take their first steps. It is a memory etched in my mind and one that forces a smile when I think of it. It took some coaxing and encouragement as they clumsily tried to lift themselves up from a crawling position and made an attempt to walk.

I don't recall the process exactly, but I'm pretty sure we did not tell them how disappointed we were that it was taking so long for them to learn a simple process that the rest of the world easily mastered. "What is wrong with you?!! *Walk!* OMG. I can't believe this. Just put one foot in front of the other. Look at your brother. He got it a long time ago. Okay, this is your last attempt. If you don't get it this time, you're crawling to school."

You laugh, but this is how most adult people talk to themselves when they start something new. They become their own worst enemy, and each time they build a little momentum, they just throw a wet verbal blanket of negative self-talk on top of the little glowing amber that could just as easily become a raging fire, if nourished and cultivated properly.

Today, I am teaching my youngest child how to drive and that brings a whole new level of emotional excitement to the job of parenting. And once again, I try to point out what she is doing well while, unemotionally, bringing attention to the subtle difference between the gas pedal and the break.

The Good News Is That It's Bad News

Both momentum and attitude are something we generate inside our mind based on evidence we see on the outside, in the world around us. And mostly, it is up to us what we choose to see, how we interpret what we see and the meaning we attach to it. But really, nothing around us has any meaning. It is all made up and we can just as easily "see" the outline of the New York City skyline as we can a blank canvas on which we can draw our own interpretation of it.

So as we look to build momentum, we should consider what we allow to enter our mind. The news media thrives on disaster. Anything bad that happens in the world is what, ultimately, sells periodicals and gets people to tune in at 11:00 for more. So for the news business, bad news is good news. Even Facebook, that was once a place where you saw the pictures of your friend's adorable children and kitten videos, is now showcasing deadly car crashes, beheadings, fist fights, and every other lewd and despicable act that could be captured on a cell phone video and posted for the world to see, with the next trying to out-do the last. The world's trash conveniently brought to your door and systematically deposited in your beautiful mind via high speed internet.

The more we expose ourselves to this negativity, the more we dilute those tenuous threads of momentum as we try to grasp some evidence that we are headed in the right direction and that our enterprise is doing well and is about to go to the next level.

You Can't Choose Your Family; but You Can Choose Whether to Invite Them to Dinner

I've always said that feedback is the breakfast of champions. It's important to get a reality-check every so often to make sure you are on track and there's no train barreling behind you. So every so often, I would ask the people whose opinion I value, a few questions that would permit a glimpse into some blind-spot that I may not even be aware exists.

"What is it about me that works?" I would ask those closest to me. "And what is a quality that can use some improvement?" These are some simple, yet very powerful, questions that can provide empowering insight, and a world of crucially-important data.

When I ran my auto repair business, a customer once stoically said, "Your prices are too high, your service sucks, and the place looks like a dump," as a reply to a similar inquiry. It was a bit too honest, but it opened my eyes to what was clear to everyone around me, but I just could not see.

On the other hand, there are some family members that make it a point, every time they see you, to put you down, joke sarcastically at your expense, make fun of your efforts and plant the seeds of doubt in your mind. Perhaps that is why we call them "family" and not "friends". Since for the most part, our friends are those people we choose to spend time with because we have similar values, goals and views of the world. They are the ones who encourage us when we're down, cry with us when we hurt, celebrate when we win, and are always there to lend a helping hand. Even when offering some painful perspective, it's done constructively and with love. There is nothing more valuable than a good, honest friend and nothing more burdensome than a cantankerous, bombastic relative.

It is the fortunate person who has relatives who they can also call friends, and if that happens to be you, this may be a good time to give them a call and tell them how much you love and appreciate them. And if not, then call and tell them that dinner is canceled.

Hard Work Never Killed Anyone; but Why Tempt It?

All my life, I've heard that if I work hard I will succeed. I've also heard that if you're doing it in more than forty hours per week, you're doing it wrong. I've seen people who worked hard make a fortune and I've seen those who worked at least as hard who could not even make bail. The infamous sign above Auschwitz promised that "work will set you free" and the one in your office says: "Hard work pays off later. Laziness pays off now".

Of course, we need to put some effort behind our goals; but simply working hard is not *the* answer, but *an* answer. There are some other pieces to the puzzle that we need to consider. Creativity is an important quality that some of the world's most successful and effective people depend on more than simply putting one's hand to the plow. (Or nose to the figurative grindstone.) In fact, to cultivate creativity, we need time away from the proverbial field so that we can re-imagine our entire endeavor. We must be rested and distracted. Time alone, surrounded by beauty, without the noise of the world buzzing all around your head, is crucial. The constantly ringing cell phone in your pocket, an avalanche of emails, and all the demands and pressures of everyday life pressing on your esophagus can make one both very busy and entirely ineffective. Getting away from all that can create a powerful context for your best ideas.

As after a heavy downpour, the earth needs some time to absorb all the water sitting in deep puddles on top. Similarly, you and I need some time to back off from all the overwhelming stimulation of modern living and give our mind time to assimilate the world around us as we take a step to the side and squat down to get a different perspective and a view of our life and work from a new angle.

Don't See What Is; Create What Could Be

The biggest deterrence to building momentum is the reality of the situation we see in front of us in the moment. Trying to get a new enterprise off the ground is probably the most difficult thing you will ever attempt. And between the financial pressures, slow drip of new customers, daily challenges, bureaucratic regulations, unexpected expenses, personnel issues, and the self-imposed, mind-numbing stress, we become a victim of the situation rather than its master. Your greatest power, however, is the ability to create a vision in your mind that will help loosen the ropes of doubt and give you the courage necessary to act, as you move through the inevitable obstacles and towards the goal you create in your imagination. And think of it this way: if it was easy, it would not have stirred your passion or consideration.

The very process of visualizing the next step creates motivation and momentum as you ascend to the higher tier and get ever closer to your goal.

What will your endeavor look like three years from now? A year is not nearly enough time to get any meaningful results. Ten years is a bit far, but three to five years is a great place to look forward to. It's kind of like hiking in the woods. We look below our feet to make sure there is nothing to trip us up, and at the same time, we look forward as far as the line of sight permits to make sure the road is taking us where we want to go. Then when we get there, we can see further. But what is the ultimate destination? Home? A special place with a beautiful view? A camp ground? This climactic target we must keep as a clear picture in our mind's eye so as to engage our goal-seeking mechanism and create the necessary motivation to keep us moving forward.

So what is your ultimate goal? Why did you start this project in the first place? What was missing in your life that you felt compelled to change it? What does its perfect outcome look like? And how will you know when you succeeded in accomplishing what you set out to do?

If you are planning to work hard, answering these questions is a very good place to start. It's not exactly back-breaking work, but it does take something to sit down and think them through. It's crucial to take the time to enter the final destination into your mental GPS so as to create the inner drive necessary to propel you forward.

Time to Grow

Once a young fella pushed his old Buick to my shop and asked if we could help get it started. One of my best mechanics came out and walked around the aged, sky blue sedan. He looked under the hood, smelled the tail pipe, put his hand on the radiator, and then hit the fender with his fist, making a noise loud enough to startle the owner. And to everyone's surprise, the car started.

"Wow!" exclaimed the owner of the now-purring car in amazement. "How much do I owe you?"

"That will be $100," answered the tech nonchalantly.

"What?! I was right here. All you did was hit the car. How would you break that down?" He said crossly.

Sure. Hitting the car took one second: $1.00. Knowing where to hit it, took a lifetime: $99.00.

It takes time to know where to hit it; and in business and marketing, it is crucial to grow and develop your expertise and understanding of the basics. That is why I think it's imperative for the healer of the future (or any new entrepreneur) to get a good grasp on both. And since this topic is not thoroughly addressed in medical school—and perhaps not at all—it has to become a personal pursuit, allocating an hour per day to read the works of some of the most effective and successful people in business, sales and marketing. So that you are not just working hard, but are extremely effective in creating the desired result with minimum effort; so that you know exactly where to hit it, so to speak.

There are many books on the topic and some of my favorites are: *Think and Grow Rich* by Napoleon Hill, *How to Win Friends and Influence People* by Dale Carnegie, *As a Man Thinketh* by James Allen, *Start With Why* by Simon Sinek, *The 22 Immutable Laws of Marketing* by Al Ries & Jack Trout, *To Sell is Human* by Daniel H. Pink, *SPIN Selling* by Neil Rackham, *The Greatest Salesman in the World* by Og Mandino, *Made to Stick* by Chip Health and Dan Heath, *The Tipping Point* by Malcom Gladwell, and *Your Marketing Sucks* by Mark Stevens. These are great places to begin gathering the fundamentals of being more effective in your business development efforts.

You Can't Hit a Target That Does Not Exist

Brady Ellison, at just 19 years old, is ranked as the world's best archer. He is able to consistently hit a two-inch target with his arrow from some 229 feet, just short of the length of a football field. But what would happen if we spun him around and removed the target? Would he be able to hit it then? Of course not. No matter how capable he may be, it is impossible to hit a target that does not exist. Similarly, you may have all the abilities in the world, but if you do not have a goal to aim for, you will never be able to hit it.

What about if we placed the target a bit further—say one mile? Or we placed it just ten feet away from the archer? In the prior case, it is unrealistically too far and we would not even bother to try, and in the latter one it would be way too easy and hardly worth the effort. So the goal we set should challenge our abilities, allow us to stretch to the next level, yet be at least within the realm of possibility for us to be able to believe that we can achieve it, less our efforts are frustrated and momentum falls like an arrow made of stone and shot by a toddler.

Setting a challenging, yet realistic goal, writing it down, visualizing it repeatedly, and keeping it at the forefront of your mind is imperative in being able to hit your target. To achieve what you are out to accomplish, it really helps when you know what that is, so that you can know when you've done it. More than anything else, that helps build momentum, optimism and confidence.

Do It for the Gipper

When my daughter was about five, she got her first two-wheel bicycle. We spent weeks in front of the house, trying to teach her how to ride it. And as long as I held on to the back of the seat, she was fine; but as soon as I let go, she'd fall to the side. It was difficult to explain the fundamentals of riding verbally; I mean, what could you possibly say? Pedal faster. Look forward. Think Lance Armstrong.

Finally, after innumerable attempts, she got it. As she took off down the block, it quickly became clear that we did not cover the "how to stop" part of the riding lesson. So I ran after her at a pace that certainly broke some kind of world record.

Once she got balance, however, she got it. No longer did it need to be taught or explained. And for the rest of her life, she will be able to get on a bicycle and ride it, even if it's years since she rode last.

As entrepreneurs, we are mostly learning balance by ourselves. Few people who are not also in business can understand us, make constructive suggestions and help us get balance in the many areas where we need it.

One of the most valuable things any independent business person should consider then is to engage a coach—Someone who can help you think things through, help you discover opportunities you may not have noticed, keep you on track, encourage you, hold you accountable, get you out of your own mind, and help you maintain the momentum necessary to reach the next level.

We see the benefits of a good coach in sports all the time, where the right person can lead an average team to victory by providing them with inspiration, philosophy of achievement, motivation, sometimes a whipping (simply repeating back what you said you're going to do but are not doing.) A coach can help you get more out of yourself than you can on your own and any additional expense will come back multiplied. Tony Robins, renowned personal development expert and bestselling author of *Awaken the Giant Within* will charge one million dollars per year to be your coach, and if you can afford it, it will probably be some of the best money you'll ever spend.

If money is a little tight just now, however, and an extra million is hard to come by, there are lots of business coaches out there, who have actually gone to school to learn how to help you be more effective and successful, and usually they will work with you for a few hundred dollars a month.

Simply knowing what to do does not guarantee that we are going to do it. A good coach can become a crucially important member of our team in helping us actually do the things we know we should be doing, but somehow always leave on the backburner. A coach can guide us through those moments of inertia and help us get out of our own way to build momentum and then hold on to it.

When 2 Plus 2 Equals 5

There is something very powerful when like-minded people get together and brainstorm ideas. Once the group develops a level of trust, mutual respect and likeability, it generates another mind that is bigger and more powerful than the sum of its parts. The Jewish religion has something called a *Minyan*. When a group of ten men gather to pray, they believe the divine mind dwells among them.

So creating a positive group that can meet on a regular basis (to help stimulate creativity and allow for the creation of something much larger than one can do on their own) is a worthwhile endeavor. In fact, it was a group like this that helped me come up with the original idea for the Health Media Group. There were a total of four of us—all entrepreneurs who were born in Russia and came to the United States as children. We would gather monthly, and in the midst of some laughs (and a little wine) we would help each other think through ideas and support one another in the endeavors that we were involved with at the time.

Here's a Little Song I Wrote; You Might Want to Sing It Note for Note

I've been going to the gym for most of my adult life, and over the years, the facilities have grown larger and the equipment more complicated. Personally, I keep it simple, using mostly free weights in the gym and my cardio I do outside as I run through the neighborhood.

Every so often, I've seen someone who was new to the fitness environment come in apprehensively, select some complex-looking machine and begin using it in a manner that it was clearly not intended. At times, it could be fairly comical and others, somewhat dangerous. But however it's used, the machine does not care either way.

Our imagination is kind of like that. It is a mechanical tool that we can use creatively to support our goals; or, we can just as easily use it to build doubt, fear and worry. Worry is not a constructive state and will do nothing to support your efforts. In fact, it can become paralyzing as you consider all the things that can go wrong: visualize the expressions on the faces of people who told you so, the repo man coming for your car in vivid color and moments detail, and your children going hungry as they look at you despondently with tears welling up in their innocent eyes—and all because you took a risk. It's kind of like sitting on a rowing machine backwards, doing sit-ups, while holding the handlebar with your teeth.

Sir William Osler, a Canadian physician and one of the founders of Johns Hopkins Hospital said, "Banish the future; live only for the moment and its allotted Work." Although it's very good advice (and a much better idea than creating a disempowering view of the future or coloring the present with all the failures of the past), I think that crafting an inspiring story that we can live into and bring into fruition is even better. It has the power to energize the moment and allow us to do those things necessary to make sure that success is inevitable.

In his book, *How to Stop Worrying and Start Living*, Dale Carnegie gives a very practical idea about how to approach worry. A modern ship has water-tight iron sections that are sealed off in the event there is damage to the hull, and the vessel begins to take on water. Similarly, Carnegie recommends that we should live in day-tight compartments, where we close off the past and the future, focusing all of our attention at the moment we are living in currently, from the second we awake to when our head hits the pillow and we fall asleep. Because if not for this moment, what is there? What is as real, as tangible and holds all the power of our ability to make an impact, than right *now*?

The late Christopher Reeve, a renowned actor who played the comic book hero *Superman* in the famed trilogy, shares a story in his book *It's Still Me* about the accident that paralyzed him from the neck down and was, ultimately, responsible for his passing.

During an equestrian competition in Culpeper, Virginia, Reeve was navigating his horse, a 12-year-old thoroughbred named Buck, over some of the hurdles set up in the large arena. As he was approaching one of the simpler obstacles towards the end of the course, his mind was focused on the final and much more difficult jump. Headed full speed ahead, committing himself fully physically, his body was there, but his mind was not. As he got ready for what was to be just another jump, the horse suddenly stopped, sending him flying head first. The full weight of his body crushed the first and second vertebrae, as his head hit the ground vertically, paralyzing him from the neck down and making his breathing and life completely dependent on machinery from that moment on.

Later reflecting on this life-shattering accident, Reeve said that, as an actor, he had spent his whole life learning to live in the moment, and here his attention was separated from his body and it was this distraction that he, ultimately, feels was responsible for the tragic outcome.

So developing the ability to live in the moment, putting some effort behind our goals, creating an inspiring vision of the future, while focusing our attention on the blessings permeating our life, is how we can best keep the angry wolves of worry at bay as we stoke the engine of momentum.

The Price Is Right . . . I Think

How much should I charge for my services? What should be the cost I set for the product I sell? Mathematically, it's not difficult to calculate. First, you determine how much it costs to manufacture the widget, then you add the expense of letting people know it exists. You estimate how many you will sell in a given time and then price it accordingly. So if it costs, say $35 to manufacture, adding a 10 or 20% profit seems reasonable, making the final price about $40.

If, however, our goal is to build momentum then this very practical approach may not be the best recipe. In the beginning, I think the prices need to be lowered sufficiently enough to make the point of entry so low that it becomes virtually irresistible for the early adopters to try.

If you would picture a bell curve, the very first people to try anything new are called innovators, those folks who stand on line to get the very latest iDevice a few months after they got the last one, and the curve ends with the laggards, those who still use a flip-phone to make their calls and insist on getting on the internet via a dial up.

When I first began producing our health and wellness events some ten years ago, I did not follow this very good advice. At that time, I just came off a dreadful partnership that left me a million dollars in debt and with a suffocating overhead. So I set my prices pretty high for anyone who wanted to participate either as an exhibitor, sponsor or attendee. And although the event grew and did relatively well in a robust economy, it never hit that critical mass of going from the innovator to the early and late majorities, allowing it to tip the scales in a way that every new business counts on if they plan to succeed at any level worth mentioning.

Today, I encourage anyone I work with to strive for the perfect environment so as to assure their schedule is full to capacity. If that takes creating a ridiculously low, below cost, loss-leader fee, then so be it. And if that is not enough, then I suggest you speak to all the companies you work with currently and get them to offer some added value to your potential clients. If there is a vitamin D supplement that you recommend people take, for example, and a particular company that manufactures it is what you naturally use because you think it's the very best on the market, then ask them to give you a few cases and give them away at your lectures, events and to all new patients who come in to your office. If you have a book, give it away for free to everyone who attends your lectures; give it to every new client and prospect. If you don't have a book, then you should sit down and write one. Meanwhile, find a book written by someone who has a similar philosophy and message, call the publisher and order a few cases at wholesale and then give those away.

Over twenty years ago, I attended a lecture by two very interesting and slightly eccentric guys who had just published their first book. After the presentation, they gave a free copy of the book to everyone in the tiny audience, and then asked us for ideas on how to best promote it. When I suggested a few organizations that I belonged to at the time, they also signed books to each of the leaders and gave them to me as well. Today Jack Canfield and Mark Victor Hansen have sold over 500 million of their *Chicken Soup for the Soul books.*

The point I'm trying to make is that to build the fire of momentum, you have to grow it and feed it as generously as you would the engine of a coal-fired locomotive. Throw away common sense and practicality and fan the flames of your endeavor with abandon. Start with a little spark; add some paper, then little, thin branches. Once you have a nice foundational fire, throw some logs on top. Don't just sit there and complain about the size of the flame on the match, as it's about to burn your fingers and flicker out. Use it to start an engulfing blaze, one that can be seen from space.

Something to think about: *You can start the world's biggest fire with the world's smallest spark.*

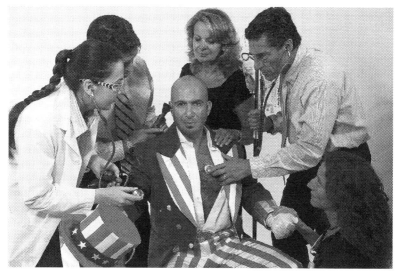

Natalie Cher, DO, Jonathan Dashiff, MD, Rita Linchitz,
RN, Richard Linchitz, MD & Mary-Beth Charno,
Certified Holistic Oncology RN, NP-S

Dr. Leonard Coldwell, bestselling author of 'The Only Answer to Cancer'
speaking at a Nutrition, Aesthetics, Vitality, Efficacy, Life (NAVEL) expo

Suzanne Somers, bestselling author of 'Ageless: the naked truth about Bioidentical Hormones' and renowned Wellness Advocate speaking at a Nutrition, Aesthetics, Vitality, Efficacy, Life (NAVEL) expo

Dr. Jeffry Life, bestselling author of The Life Plan: Dr. Life's Guide for Men to Great Health, Better Sex & a Stronger, Leaner Body' speaking at a Nutrition, Aesthetics, Vitality, Efficacy, Life (NAVEL) expo

JJ Virgin, bestselling author of 'The Virgin Diet: Why Food Intolerance is the Real Cause of Weight Gain' speaking at a Nutrition, Aesthetics, Vitality, Efficacy, Life (NAVEL) expo

Kevin Trudeau, bestselling author of "Natural Cures 'They' Don't Want Your to Know About speaking at a Nutrition, Aesthetics, Vitality, Efficacy, Life (NAVEL) expo

Chapter 10

Healthy Perseverance

If you really believe in what you're doing, work hard, take nothing personally and if something blocks one route, find another. Never give up." — *Laurie Notaro, Author*

If I wanted to make some real money, I tell people who ask, I'd open up a chain of liquor stores. But somehow I stumbled into this wellness side of the health care industry, and it became a passion that has absorbed me fully. Perhaps I'm more an ideologue than entrepreneur—one who believes in people's potential for unlimited achievement, the idiom that the good guys always win, and absolutely despises the something-for-nothing mentality, aka Dudley, the Entitled Muggle Paradigm, in all its forms. So when I saw just how bureaucratic, skewed and dysfunctional health care is in this nation, it made me mad and I wanted to make a difference. Perhaps that is not the best business plan, but surely if everyone just did the profitable thing instead of the right thing, we would have never survived as a species.

Along the way I've had my doubts, primarily because I never worked so hard at anything, putting everything on the line, and it seemed like every evil force in the world was out to derail my efforts, discourage my spirit and have me simply leave and go do something else. But it's difficult to quit when I've grown to love making a difference in people's lives and have seen the remarkable transformations of those who took advantage of the life-transforming information generously shared by our wellness-oriented doctors, grabbed responsibility for their health back from some nebulous entity and got their life back, sometimes, literally.

The Doctor's Gone Fishin'

It is not uncommon to hear in the uncertainty of the current environment of doctors who prefer to retire rather than continue to practice as a pawn in a game they cannot possibly win. And certainly, it's understandable. After some ten years of a very expensive education and a lifetime of serving people, few self-respecting doctors will want to subjugate themselves to some regime that has placed so many hoops for them to jump through, their feet barely having time to touch ground.

But why give up the profession you love and simply disappear into the long goodnight. Your life's work, the health of the public and one of the noblest occupations on the planet is being bastardized and taken away from you, and the only thing you can think of doing in response . . . is quit? And then, do what? Go fishing?

Certainly, this is not the first time in history where a fight is not only warranted . . . it is demanded. A big bully threw sand in your eyes, kissed your girlfriend on the lips, took your lunch money, and insulted your mother, and you're just going to go home and huffily rummage through the closet for a fishing rod? The words "I only regret I have but one life to give" come to mind. The founders of our nation had no less to lose when they signed the Declaration of Independence and pledged their lives, their fortunes and their sacred honor to a cause much bigger than any one individual. All because they felt the added tax made the price of tea a bit too hefty. Lucky, they never lived to see a Starbucks; or the compulsory decree by the federal government forcing you to purchase a sub-par product from a crony-capitalistic enterprise.

It was, however, the principle of the matter and those who breathed life into this nation were not going to stand for the continued abuses, usurpations, and the absolute Tyranny over these States by a self-serving bureaucracy. So they unanimously declared: "when in the course of human events it becomes necessary for one people to dissolve the political bands which have connected them with another and to assume among the powers of the earth, the separate and equal station to which the Laws of Nature and of Nature's God entitle them, a decent respect to the opinions of mankind requires that they should declare the causes which impel them to the separation." Never have these words rang so true as when juxtaposed with the modern day government-seized system of health care. These few brave souls, of whom three happened to be doctors, proved that indeed, not only can you fight city hall, sometimes it's the only course there is.

If anyone is to take the health care system back from the third-party bureaucrats and create a much better, more aerodynamic, affordable, logical and modern approach with a focus on wellness and prevention, I can think of no one who could do it better than the smartest, most hardworking, caring and passionate people in our society who dedicated their entire life to the art of healing.

What would your perfect health care system look like? Is it anything like it is today? I'm going to guess that if you took the time to read this book, that you are not content with the way things are, and neither are you willing to settle for the status quo. And if that's accurate, then you must do something. You have to. I'm not sure what that something is, but first you need to let go of the world as you know it and let it fall and break into a million pieces. Free yourself from the perception of reality, open your mind to the possibility that there are things you don't know, and even more that you do not know that you don't know, and it is in that darkness of the unknown that you will find the light that illuminates your authentic self. Take the red pill Neo and follow the rabbit hole.

Someone, no better than you, and perhaps with less noble motives, created the current reality of a system everyone accepts at face value, but it's nothing more than a facade like that of a town in an old Hollywood western, or some little man behind the big wizard's curtain creating a larger- than-life illusion.

Doctor, the President Will See You Now

Since 1965, with the birth of Medicare, spending for health care grew exponentially—from 6% of GDP to over 18%, stretching quickly past the yellow, three trillion dollars per year end-of-road caution sign. Over ten years ago when I first started flirting with this health and wellness industry, it was clear that the current path was simply unsustainable. As the elastic band on our cumulative stretchy-pants continued to expand to accommodate our gluttonous demand for health services (primarily paid for by someone, anyone, other than "I"), the system would have to change or the passengers on this boat that we're all on, are in danger of exceeding the maximum weight capacity, and pulling down the entire US enterprise below the ocean's surface and parking it on the deserted streets of the mythological city of Atlantis.

In 2004, our government tried to implement a stop-gap measure with the high-deductible Health Savings Accounts. This idea would permit the individual to put away pre-tax dollars in an interest earning bank account and use it for basic health services; in the case of a catastrophic health event, an insurance policy would kick in and all of the expenses would then be paid in full. This idea placed the responsibility for the basic maintenance of health, as well as the spending decisions for minor and preventive health care; in the hands of the individual.

At the same time (and it seemed coincidental), people began taking more interest in doing the things necessary for staying healthy. Organic products became readily available, vegetable juicing got really popular, supermarkets that catered to the health-conscious consumer proliferated, gyms and yoga studios began popping up on every street corner, and people got in the habit of taking vitamins, as well as visiting their chiropractor, acupuncturist, and holistic doctor more readily. During this time frame, Entenmann's (a donut, cookie and cake bakery founded in 1898) recently closed its manufacturing plant here on the Bay Shore of Long Island, Twinkies went under, Coca Cola is diversifying away from soda as sales flatten and, according to the CDC, smoking is on a precipitous decline.

Books and articles published by many experts simultaneously, all reported the same healthy trajectory. More of the responsibility for the maintenance of health will be placed in the hands of the public, they said; so the market responded enthusiastically with the products and services to accommodate this very welcome phenomenon.

Since we, at the Health Media Group, are in the business of educating people on the fundamentals of wellness, fitness, lasting beauty, anti-aging protocols, longevity and the reversal of chronic conditions using natural approaches; through events, printed publications and a radio talk show at the time, we were happily riding this wave of public interest. Our events attracted thousands of people, the exhibitor space was full past capacity, and all the 6 - 8 lecture slots per hour of the expo were full from 9 AM in the morning to 9 PM in the evening by healers, doctors and authors who were proactively out there sharing their message. Major corporations and popular media were partnering with us, and it was only a question of time till we, as a nation, hit that tipping point that would transform health care as we know it.

It was during that critical-mass stage that the current administration hit the brakes on the HSA idea of the last and put the entire health care system in the hands of the government. After over ten years of my life, and millions of dollars in investment, the entire system came to a screeching halt with a stealthy decision made by a handful of bureaucrats in some office in a land far away.

It is here, in this moment of severe adversity, when the situation is clearly out of our control that we will choose to either persist or quit. The exact definition of perseverance is: *steadfastness in doing something despite difficulty or delay in achieving success.* Yes, but it is also slaying the dragons of doubt in your own mind. It is creating a clear vision of how you want things to go, and it is building a phalanx of support around you of inspirational people who encourage you and help you identify opportunities in the challenges of the moment. The kind of people who give you the courage to move beyond the current pain to that place where the planets align and your surfboard hits the perfect wave.

In Napoleon Hill's classic book *Think and Grow Rich*, the author shares a story about a gold prospector who went to seek his fortunes in the mud of California. After finding what looked like evidence of a fertile mine, he went back and raised money for equipment and man-power to cultivate it. At first, his hunch proved accurate and buckets of gold were brought to the surface, quickly returning his investment. Just as he was about to hit the big profits, the only thing the mine birthed was dirt. After exerting more effort that was rewarded with more frustration, he sold all the equipment to a local junk man, and went home dispirited and empty handed.

The junk man however, hired an engineer, who examined the mine and explained that the project failed because the previous team was not familiar with fault lines. And after some calculation, he suggested the vain of gold could be picked up just three feet from where the other vein ended. And that is exactly where it was—just a few feet stood between the original founder of the mine and one of the richest gold discoveries of the time.

Perseverance then is continually looking beyond the fault line for your vein of gold, knowing that if you just continue looking, if you let go of the possibility of it not being there, that sooner or later if you continue to seek ye shall find, or if not it, you will find something even better.

Although I've spent the last few years in the dark lugubriousness of my own fault-line, recent events in the political arena are showing some glimmer of hope that may very well be the tail of the next vein of opportunity one much larger than the last. The pendulum, it seems, is about to swing the other way and health care will be placed back in the hands of the consumer where it ultimately belongs. But even if I'm wrong, one thing I know for sure is that I will keep looking, digging, thinking, asking and trying; I will never stop until I'm riding the crescent of next wave, allowing the feeling of being alive to permeate my being.

In other words, my exit strategy . . . is death.

Fail Fast and Do It Forward

If I could start my life all over again, I would not lament all the mistakes I've made, all the money I lost and all the dumb things I've done. I would just do them faster. I would condense a decade of mistakes into a year. I would not look back and fear another stumble; I would move forward and learn from each wrong turn. Because, ultimately, it is the proper interpretation of experience, allowing it to open its wisdom to you like the bud of a rose opens itself to the sun that is the most powerful teacher of all. Getting frozen by the fear of the unknown, labeling yourself a failure because you've failed, and being overly cautious are the greatest of all dangers. Time waits for no one and it goes by very quickly, so the opportunity not taken is an opportunity most probably lost. So don't look before you leap; leap and learn how to fly.

From Russia with Love, and Kielbasa

When we first landed at JFK airport as the final stop of our three-month immigration journey, one of the things my father attempted to smuggle in, was a Kielbasa roll the size of a teenagers arm. The other was some fairly large diamonds.

Having to hand over what was the soviet bloc's version of the nutritional pyramid to an immigration officer, was a very scary proposition for people who had no idea where their next meal would come from. My parents at the time were both in their early thirties my brother was seven, and in a few months I would celebrate my 11th birthday.

When I think back to that time I can't help but wonder what it must have been like for people like my parents to leave life as they know it and travel to a land where they did not speak the language, did not know the customs, had no friends or contacts, with a belief system that was often in direct contradiction to the realities of their new environment, only a few hundred dollars to their name and no idea what tomorrow would bring.

I can only imagine if today I was all of a sudden forced to leave my home, grab a few belongings and travel thousands of miles to China's Zhujiajiao city where I was alone, and responsible for the survival of my family. Just then I wake up in a cold sweat, my heart palpitating wildly, as I try to catch my breath, and, happily, I find myself surrounded by the life I know and have come to take for granted.

The Streets are Paved with Gold; and Gravel

My dad's full name is Roman Leonidovich Lubarsky, and back in Russia, he ran a fairly large division for the government's transportation hub in Moscow, managing hundreds of people and dealing with many of the party leaders directly.

His first job here in this new land was to unload a tractor trailer. He and another fellow spent the entire day moving hundreds of heavy boxes, with no lunch break and limited trips to the bathroom. After their long day came to an end, Dad was handed a twenty dollar bill and a cold "farewell". It was only many years later that he shared this story, for at the time, he never let on what he was going through or how difficult it was for him to adapt.

When the shipment of crates finally arrived (after some six months), we were all very excited. At long last we could put some real furniture in our one-bedroom apartment that was, till then, sparsely decorated with whatever charitable organizations were able to find for us and that the kind super of our building salvaged from the trash. My dad, however, was excited for a different reason. When packing the slightly-lopsided dining room set, made with pride in the former USSR to cross the ocean, he stealthily took off his jacket and threw it inside one of the crates. In a side pocket, he had a pill box with a couple of fairly large diamonds that were the condensed evidence of his life's work till that point and would be the springboard for his new life here.

As my mother, brother and I were busy removing the pieces we could lift from the two large wooden crates now taking up most of the living space, my dad sat quietly on the worn couch, the open pill box in his hand and his face ashen. On the long journey from one world to the next, the diamonds never made it.

Ooo La La Sasoon; By Roman

The very first endeavor my dad got involved with was selling knock-off jeans—ones that he knocked off to the stores on Delaney Street in Manhattan's downtown (near the Williamsburg Bridge and surrounding areas). As a kid I remember jeans stacked up to the ceiling in the living room of our one-bedroom apartment, creating a blue maze for us kids to play in, constantly tattooing the cheap coloring onto the tips of our fingers.

Having purchased the labels and tags, as well as the machines from China that we used to adhere the newly logo'd buttons to the front and the metal tags to the back pocket, there was a virtual assembly line occupying every inch of our living space; one that grew as more relatives arrived from the former mother land. Within a few months, we opened a small retail store in the South Bronx. I would stand there as a mature pre-teen in front of the entrance with a table piled high with our merchandise and entice the passersby to take a look as strands of Merengue blared from an open window of someone's apartment nearby and a group played a shell game atop of some boxes in front of the pharmacy next door.

Once two grown men came up, one who stood in front of me blocking my view as the other grabbed a couple of jeans and hid them under his jacket. I would have never known if a Good Samaritan did not immediately tell me what happened. By the time I caught up with them, they were a block away nonchalantly standing in some doorway. As I looked down, the jeans were lying in a corner behind them. I pushed passed them, grabbed my property, and without looking at the two adult hooligans, went back to my post, not giving it another thought.

During the first year of the store, it was broken into three times. Once they crawled through the back window. Another time, they cut the locks on the front door. Finally, they broke into the basement of the pharmacy next door, made a hole in the concrete wall separating the two buildings and pulled out most of the merchandise leaving a few pieces hanging on the newly-made Shawshank-like tunnel, with the alarm doing little more than adding to the ambient sounds of city living as it lulled people to sleep.

Once again, Dad was back on the worn couch, not a pair of jeans to be found, and his face ashen.

Hail, the Taxi

Once he got behind the wheel of a taxi, we hardly saw him. Dad worked from five in the morning to late at night every day of the week. In the early 80's with a small down payment, one could purchase a yellow taxi medallion for a reasonable thirty thousand dollars. As soon as he figured it out and had enough saved to do it, he began buying medallions as fast as possible. Within a few years, his fleet grew to 24 yellow cabs; at their peak, valued at a million dollars each.

All these cars in New York City presented numerous problems of where to park them when not in use and where to affordably maintain this fleet. So against the advice of everyone who knew him, Dad placed a down payment on a five thousand square foot, one-story building on

Seventeenth Street between Ninth and Tenth Avenues today probably worth 20 times its original value. The cars that could be hacked-up back then and used as taxi's had to be one of the big three American automakers, with the Dodge being more popular because of its lower price, I suppose. Those cars, however, did not fare well under the tremendous demands of the unforgiving New York streets, and you could often find them standing on the side of the road with a blown engine, a non-responsive transmission or with flames shooting from under the hood; once one of our cars literally snapped in half with the chassis (the steel frame undercarriage around which the car was assembled) stuck in the asphalt of the Grand Central Parkway.

Purchasing parts for these cars from the dealer was prohibitively expensive. Trying to get them from the junk yards would cost a tremendous amount of time, and you never knew if the part was good and if the car would be able to go back to work after you spent the day installing the motor you hauled back from Hunts Point auto salvage.

There was also Shlomo, the Junk Man, who drove around in a white box truck and delivered difficult-to-find parts at very reasonable rates. So if one needed an engine for a 1981 Dodge Diplomat, for example—a vehicle also used by the New York City detectives—you would call Shlomo who would rarely disappoint.

It was in the early hours of a lovely spring day, when about ten of those unmarked Dodge Diplomats descended on our little world. They came from every direction, sirens blaring, tires screeching and doors slamming, as dozens of *Starsky and Hutch* lookalikes ran towards Dad's building with their guns drawn and the badges hung around their necks swinging.

In America, it seems, the law frowns on when someone steals police cars, takes them to a chop-shop and then sells off the parts to the highest bidder. Go figure. Since all the transactions were done in cash and the receipts pretty generic. My dad was the one who was arrested. Besides, he would never give anyone up to save himself. It's just how we roll.

Please Talk into the Mic

Although he received a relative slap on the wrist with a five--year probation, the process was very expensive and he lost the shop on Seventeenth Street. So we moved to Forty-Seventh Street and Eleventh Avenue. The space was a one-story building the size of an average warehouse that we rented from a former citizen of the USSR who now owned a number of buildings in Manhattan, drove a relatively new Rolls Royce and wore green blazers and matching loafers with no sox.

Things were getting back to normal. We expanded our business to two tow trucks, a body shop and an auto repair business. Our office was built like the bedroom of a loft—on top of the back wall of the space with a single staircase going up to it, and through the office window you could see all the goings on in the work area below.

That day when I walked into the office, I saw a familiar face talking to my dad who was sitting behind his desk. The person he was speaking with was an agent from the Taxi Limousine Commission. At the time, this was a fairly new government agency that was more like an accounting department than enforcement and not taken very seriously by the industry. So because Dad did not speak English well and did not understand all the paperwork needed to run his fleet of yellow cabs, he would 'tip' these men in black to take care of any papers that needed updating.

On the tape we heard later, you could hear my displeasure (expressed with emphasis, in superlatives and in Russian) upon seeing this uniformed representative. It seems this agency was on a witch hunt, and so this day, the agent (who recently found his way back to the work force from the rolls of public assistance) came to collect forty dollars for getting my dad some license for one of the cars that he could just as easily have gotten himself in all of ten minutes if he had the inclination to drive to the TLC office in midtown.

A month or so later, an unmarked Dodge Diplomat was standing in front of our apartment building waiting for Dad to come out and go to work. The deal was fairly simple: Give us one of the big fish within the TLC and we'll let you go. Needless to say, Dad took the 2-5 year option in a minimum-security federal resort near the Canadian border that came with some free Chinese food, purchased by one of the detectives duly impressed by dad's unwillingness to snitch.

In short order, and on my 16th birthday, a swarm of TLC agents stumbled to our new shop down 47th Street like a bunch of zombies from a bad version of the Michael Jackson *Thriller* video, and with a chisel and hammer, removed all the medallions from the hoods of a sea of yellow cabs that drove up for the five PM shift change.

And here, once again, Dad was back on the proverbial worn couch with an ashen face . . . only this time . . . it was on Riker's Island.

There are No Happy Endings . . . Just Happy Travels

It took about a week for Dr. Jeffrey Salz and his guide to climb the 11,020 foot high Mt. Fitz Roy located near El Chalten village in the Southern Patagonian Ice Field in Patagonia (on the border between Argentina and Chile). Dr. Salz has a PhD in cultural anthropology. He is the author of *The Way of Adventure: Transforming Your Life and Work with Spirit and Vision* and is one of the most memorable and impactful speakers I've ever heard.

On this particular trip, as he related the story at an event I attended some 15 years ago, they spent their days climbing the icy mountain wall and their nights attached to it as they tried to sleep suspended high above the village below. Throughout the trip, they had to develop a trust for each other where they literally placed their life in the hands of their climbing partner. There were challenges to overcome, lessons to learn, fear to conquer, winds to contend with, cold to bear, a goal to focus on and a mission to accomplish. It took a full day for them to descend from the mountain's zenith where they paused for a quick photo. As they were walking away from this conquered rock, dragging all the equipment behind them, exhausted, wind-burned, disheveled, and proud of their achievement, they encountered a young local boy. "Where are you from?" He asked, staring at them curiously, wide-eyed and unblinking. "We are from the top of that mountain," they answered, cocking their heads toward the snow-covered peak that penetrated the clouds above. After pausing for a moment, the boy said bewildered: "But there is nothing on top of that mountain."

And so, there is only the life we live, the people we grow to love and trust, and what our goals allow us to become; and not so much the goals themselves that makes up both success and life itself. Because, there is nothing on top of that figurative, or literal mountain, and most of all, that is what my dad taught me through his trials and tribulations, his failures and successes, his courage, tenacity and stiff upper lip. Life is a journey and there is no 'there' to get to for it is already here. Through his actions, Dad taught me that success is the ability to go from one failure to another without loss of enthusiasm. Later, another great man from across the pond put this powerful idea into words.

Roman Leonidovich Lubarsky finally found his fortune back in Russia. As the USSR fell apart, many of his old contacts became oligarchs and there were plenty of opportunities for him to take advantage of in a land that he better understood, with a language he spoke without an accent, and where government employees more readily appreciated his generous overtures.

Gritty Brit: Forged Between the Hammer of Evil and the Anvil of Good

Perhaps the greatest example of perseverance was born in the worst of time for the world and its people. When Nazi forces were threatening the world with slavery or extermination, there were few willing to stand up to this seemingly unbeatable force. When they first began flexing their military muscle, their chancellor with the Brazilian bikini mustache would call on the neighboring nations and simply threaten them with annihilation. "If you do not surrender," he said to Poland, arms flailing and spit flying, "We will send our troops, our planes and our tanks, and will permanently remove your country from the map." That threat seemed sufficient for most to open their borders and allow the goose-stepping, flag waving, swastika-wearing troops to enter triumphantly and completely take over the country and subjugate its people.

He continued the same successful sales pitch with Austria, Belgium, France, Romania, Yugoslavia, Greece, and many others who all chose to surrender rather than fight a losing battle. Everything was going as planned, until this intense 'Puss in Boots' called on Winston Churchill, who was then the Prime minister of England, and repeated his, thus-far-unchallenged threat. "If you do not surrender, we will bomb your tiny nation into oblivion." For all intents and purposes, that should have been enough to supine Churchill and add another nation-trophy to the tyrant's mantle.

But Churchill's answer was unequivocal, delivered I suppose in that sonorous voice with a tinge of electric fury: "We shall fight [you] on the seas and oceans, we shall fight [you] in the air, we shall fight on the beaches, we shall fight on the landing grounds, we shall fight in the fields and in the streets, we shall fight in the hills; we shall never surrender."

Many historians believe that this one man was responsible for igniting the world to unite and stamp out the evil forces of his time that threatened to set the world ablaze. And even today, some seven decades later, his words continue to inspire us to pursue greatness, to challenge brutality, and to fight for freedom no matter the cost.

So, What's the Point?

Many years later, Sir Winston Churchill was invited to deliver the commencement address at Oxford University. The lecture room was filled to capacity by a thousand bright faces of the next generation, eager to learn the secrets to life, perseverance in the face of seemingly insurmountable challenges, and accomplishing the impossible when the world is telling you that it can't be done and that you can't do it.

As my favorite interpretation of the story goes, Winston Churchill finally mounted the stage and approached the podium still dressed as if he were walking in a London park during a rainy day. As more of the audience became aware of his presence, the room instinctively lowered its volume to mute. All eyes focused on the figure they were there to see. Some became emotional at the very thought of what this one man stood for and the remarkable accomplishment that was his life.

There he was in front of a standing-room-only crowd in his hat and rain coat, dangling an umbrella off his left forearm and holding a lit cigar in the fingers of his right hand. At this point, you could probably hear an eye blink, or if you prefer, a pin drop, as he took off his hat and placed it on top of the podium in front and hung his umbrella on its side.

Then, after what seemed like an eternity, he quietly said:

"Never, never, give up."

He put the cigar back in his mouth and took a hearty drag. After a few seconds of eternal silence, he once again and more forcefully repeated:

"Never, never, give up!"

The sound of his voice echoed through the halls of this learning institution, etching themselves on the marbled walls and on the people's hearts. He placed the cigar back in his mouth for another puff. The audience looked up in pregnant anticipation, as he fired the final incantation with the force of a man made up of the solid bronze of pure belief:

"NEVER, NEVER GIVE UP!" he belted as he put his hat back on his head, replaced the umbrella on his left forearm and quietly headed for the exit.

Something to think about: *Be bold and audacious; for when you get to the end of your life, you will regret the things you did not do more than the ones you did.*

Conclusion

This has been quite a ride. I've enjoyed it immensely up until this point and am very much looking forward to seeing a market-driven system of health care emerge in this nation that is accessible to everyone who needs it and wants it; a system where doctors are free to bring more art and creativity to healing and at the same time embrace entrepreneurship and the art of selling their message to the huddled masses yearning to be well. But, no matter how flush or vast our system of care, it will always be limited if the people themselves are not willing to take some control and responsibility for their health and wellbeing. It is up to us then, as the creators of a new approach to the health and wellness industry to teach, inspire and encourage the three hundred million people who live in this nation, to see the value in the maintenance of, and investment in, their most valuable possession.

If you are so inclined, please untangle yourself from all third-party payers. Create a practice that is on your terms and based on a philosophy that you believe deep in your soul will be the best approach to help people heal at the very root of their underlying problem. Once you develop a message that resonates with people, sit down and write a book about it. Put yourself in front of as many people as opportunity permits, and coach them on how to stay well for a lifetime. All you need to live a prosperous and happy life, is a few hundred of the right kind of clients / patients.

There is nothing wrong with this health care system that a relatively small group of passionate people cannot re-imagine and re-engineer. The public has never been more with you. They have never been more frustrated with the status quo medicine that does not take the time to understand what is causing their symptoms, and simply stuffs the only tangible evidence of an underlying problem behind the door of a closet so full it's ready to explode. Or the heavy-handed intrusion by the government into the intimate relationship between doctor and patient.

To find a marketing platform that suits you best, try numerous approaches. Build your presence and don't be afraid to make the necessary investments. Drug companies spend more money on promoting their products than they do for research and development. A lot more. Put your money to work for you. Let your dollars go searching for the perfect next patient. One who will be the source of a hundred new patients through the word-of-mouth they create after they experience your personalized, attentive and results-based brand of healing.

Keep the flow of new patients taut and steady. Don't let up. It is easier to raise your prices or take on an associate who will contend with the overflow than try to get the momentum back once it falters.

I have been really inspired by the courage of so many doctors who are extremely vocal in their dissatisfaction with the trajectory of this government-controlled health care. It's one thing for me to voice my opinion. I don't have a medical license to consider, and if worse comes to worse, I can always start that chain of liquor stores I mentioned. Many of these physicians are literally putting it all on the line. They are throwing off the shackles that bureaucracy has tried very hard to impose on them and are recreating their approach to providing care in a way that takes their own interests into consideration. How radical. This is a crack in a façade that will, ultimately, bring this machine to a halt and have it come crumbling down so that we can, finally, see the blue sky of hope and a rainbow of renewal.

I am thrilled that you and I have been able to meet through the words of this book. I am excited for you and all the future doctors who will take health care away from third-party bureaucrats and embrace *the art of selling the art of healing.*

Acknowledgements

It only took about six months to write this book but many decades of experiences to become the person who is able to write it. I'd like to express my deepest gratitude to all of the giants in my life on whose shoulders I stand, and who have helped me evolve from a junk yard dog into a man that I can be comfortable introducing at parties.

Let me begin with my wife, Alina, who for some 25 years, stood by my side, helped me polish some of my many rougher edges, and has been the main source of inspiration in all my efforts. I adore that girl. Then there is my son, Adriel, and daughter, Bashel, who are the joy of my life, and have filled me with priceless moments of love, fun, pride, hope and meaning. They are some of my best work on this planet. Next, my mommy, Ada, who is my biggest fan and has been a supporting part in everything I've done or thought of doing. Her unwavering love and belief in me is a source of power in my life. Likewise, my dad, Roman, who strived valiantly to give his children the life he never had. He has taught me everything about work ethic, toughness, optimism and perseverance. They don't make 'em like that anymore.

This page would not be complete without an expression of gratitude to my mother-in-law. No, really. Jane Goloborodko not only gave me the gift of a lifetime in my better half, she has insisted on helping with mailings, filings, organizing and volunteering her time at each of our events for many years. She is super cool.

I'd like to thank my work partner, Kathy Ravel, who has brought a new level of inspiration to our work. Her creativity, optimism and willingness to go above and beyond the call of duty has permitted us to make strides that I could not have imagined before we met. I'd like to thank Loraine Dégraff, who is a brilliant writer and editor and has been instrumental in helping me organize my thoughts and help create the structure to bring this work to the world. I'd like to thank Ramfis Myrthil for all of his youthful enthusiasm and Alanna Garone for her great suggestions and encouragement.

They say blood is thicker than water, but that is only relevant if you live in a nest of vampires. Although there's no denying the value of family, those people who we, ultimately, call friends are cultivated over a lifetime and built on the same values, mutual respect, admiration and support of one another. My wife and I are blessed with a small army of some of the most remarkable, brilliant and beautiful people in the world that we have the privilege of knowing as friends. Most have insisted on volunteering at Health Media events and have been a source of revelations, encouragement, support, and stories (some that I've shared in these pages). I'd like to thank Steven and Luba Tabak, Alex and Ella Kaminsky, Sasha and Sashachka Kleyman, Alex and Alona Chervinsky,

Gene and Marisha Kozlov, Leny and Bella Moreyn, Sergey and Marina Khaymovich, Gary and Alla Chervinsky, Edward and Maya Shteyman, Michael and Ella Kolchinskiy, Vadim and Victoria Firdman, Abe and Inna Post, Jack and Inna Fraktas, and Edward and Irene Fruitman. Your generosity, kindness and love are priceless gifts that we value beyond measure.

A very warm "thank you" to John and Arline Simeone, my original mentors, who have lovingly set my life on a grander course and to whom I am forever indebted.

Since we spend most of our life working, being surrounded by some of the smartest, most caring and genuinely good people, is a blessing that is difficult to express. It's kind of like a kid who grew up in the slums of Calcutta and, all of a sudden, gets promoted to serve the honored guests at a royal ball. It is a gift that I treasure and an opportunity that I value like a Romanov-style crystal family heirloom.

With that, I'd like to thank all of the doctors and healers who I've had the honor of knowing over some 10 years in this field of natural health and wellness. Starting with Dr. Richard Linchitz who is, unquestionably, one of the most incredible people I have ever met. I'd like to thank Sylvie Beljanski, Dr. John Hall, Dr. Michael Berlin, Dr. Alex Schvartsman, Dr. Garry D'Brant, Dr. Chris Calapai, Dr. Kelly O'Malley Mattone, Dr. Sergey Kalitenko, Dr. Ellen Kamhi, Dr. Howard Robins, Dr. Louis Vastola, Dr. Perry Frankel, Dr. Thomas Ianiello, Dr. Moshe Dekel, Dr. Alexis Hugelmeyer, Dr. Jane Goldberg, Dr. Jesse Stoff, Dr. Bear Walker, Dr. Jonathan Dashiff, Dr. Natalie Cher, Dr. Frank Cohen, Dr. Scott Banks, Dr. Marla Friedman, Dr. Fred Blum, Drs. Roy and Dianne Speiser, Dr. Robert Matrisciano, Dr. Karen Barbosa, Dr. Fred Cohen,

Dr. John Gehnrich and Dr. Micki Gelb, as well as all the integrative, wellness-oriented healers who are helping create the future of market-driven medical care.

A very special "thank you" to Mary Mucci of News 12 TV and Long Island Naturally, who has been our Media partner from the early beginning, Neil and Andrea Garvey of *Creations Magazine*, Ray Florio of *JetSet Magazine*, Ron Russo of Clear Channel Media, as well as Kelly Martinsen and Tina Woods of *Natural Awakenings Magazine*.

I lovingly tip my hat to my friend Laura Fallon, who exhibited at our very first event and has never missed one since.

I'd like to thank my "stars", who have brought credibility, notoriety and magical pixy dust to our efforts: Suzanne Somers, Carol Alt, Kat James, Fran Drescher, Dara Torez, Kevin Trudeau, JJ Virgin, Dr. Leonard Coldwell, Cherie (the Juice Lady) Calbom, Dr. Gary Null, Dr. Bernie Siegel, Drs. Jayson and Mira Calton, Dr. Mark Hyman, Steve Rizzo, Liana Werner-Gray, and Dr. Jeffry Life.

A great big "thank you" to Stuart Scott of Mountain Valley Spring Water, Jack Bozzano of Bozzano Organic Olive Oil, John Wood of US Wellness Foods and all of the companies and sponsors who have made this work possible. Your support, trust and encouragement have allowed me to tap abilities and talents that I had no idea I had. It has stirred in me a fire to learn, grow and become more effective, and brings deep satisfaction and fulfilment to my existence.

Thank you very much to the many thousands of health-conscious people who took the time to attend our events, read our publications, and share their mostly encouraging, and at times, brutally honest feedback. You are the reason for all of this effort, and we are so grateful for your proactive interest and continued support of good health, good food and ageless, living protocols.

On behalf of all of us, I would also like to thank *you,* the person reading this book. It is my greatest hope that you will be inspired enough to take the action that will multiply your presence in the world by a thousand, that you will be willing to make mistakes and fail forward as you become a force for good as rare and powerful as the Halie's Comet, and that we and our children will benefit enormously from your greatness.

THE START.